Collins

11+
Non-Verbal Reasoning

Quick Practice Tests
Ages 9-10

Beatrix Parnaby-Price

Contents

About this book 3	Test 13 33
Test 1 4	Test 14 35
Test 2 6	Test 15 38
Test 3 9	Test 16 40
Test 4 11	Test 17 42
Test 5 13	Test 18 44
Test 6 15	Test 19 46
Test 7 17	Test 20 48
Test 8 19	Test 21 51
Test 9 22	Test 22 54
Test 10 25	Test 23 56
Test 11 27	Test 24 59
Test 12 30	Answers 63

ACKNOWLEDGEMENTS

The author and publisher are grateful to the copyright holders for permission to use quoted materials and images.

Every effort has been made to trace copyright holders and obtain their permission for the use of copyright material. The author and publisher will gladly receive information enabling them to rectify any error or omission in subsequent editions. All facts are correct at time of going to press.

Published by Collins
An imprint of HarperCollins*Publishers* Limited
1 London Bridge Street
London SE1 9GF

HarperCollins*Publishers*
Macken House
39/40 Mayor Street Upper
Dublin 1
D01 C9W8
Ireland

ISBN: 9781844199136

First published 2018
This edition published 2020
Previously published by Letts

10 9 8

British Library Cataloguing in Publication Data.

A CIP record of this book is available from the British Library.

Author: Beatrix Parnaby-Price, a tutor for Bonas MacFarlane
Series Editor: Faisal Nasim
Commissioning Editor: Michelle I'Anson
Editor and Project Manager: Sonia Dawkins
Cover Design: Kevin Robbins and Sarah Duxbury
Text and Page Design: Ian Wrigley
Layout and Artwork: Q2A Media
Production: Natalia Rebow
Printed in the UK, by Ashford Colour Press Ltd.

MIX
Paper | Supporting responsible forestry
FSC™ C007454

This book contains FSC™ certified paper and other controlled sources to ensure responsible forest management.

For more information visit: www.harpercollins.co.uk/green

About this book

Familiarisation with 11+ test-style questions is a critical step in preparing your child for the 11+ selection tests. This book gives children lots of opportunities to test themselves in short, manageable bursts, helping to build confidence and improve the chance of test success.

It contains 24 tests designed to develop key non-verbal reasoning skills.

- Each test is designed to be completed within a short amount of time. Frequent, short bursts of revision are found to be more productive than lengthier sessions.

- GL Assessment tests can be quite time-pressured so these practice tests will help your child become accustomed to this style of questioning.

- We recommend your child uses a pencil to complete the tests, so that they can rub out the answers and try again at a later date if necessary.

- Children will need a pencil and a rubber to complete the tests as well as some spare paper for rough working. They will also need to be able to see a clock/watch and should have a quiet place in which to do the tests.

- Answers to every question are provided at the back of the book, with explanations given where appropriate.

- After completing the tests, children should revisit their weaker areas and attempt to improve their scores and timings.

Download a free progress chart from our website
collins.co.uk/11plus

Test 1

You have 5 minutes to complete this test.

You have 10 questions to complete within the given time.

There are two figures on the left with an arrow between them. Decide how the second figure is related to the first.

There is then a third figure followed by an arrow and five more figures.

Decide which figure is related to the third in the same way as the first two figures are related. Circle the letter below it.

EXAMPLE

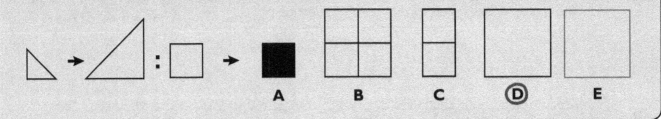

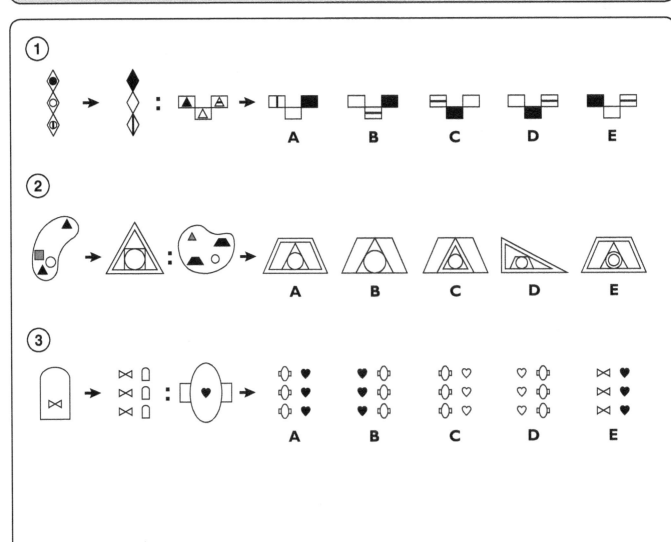

4

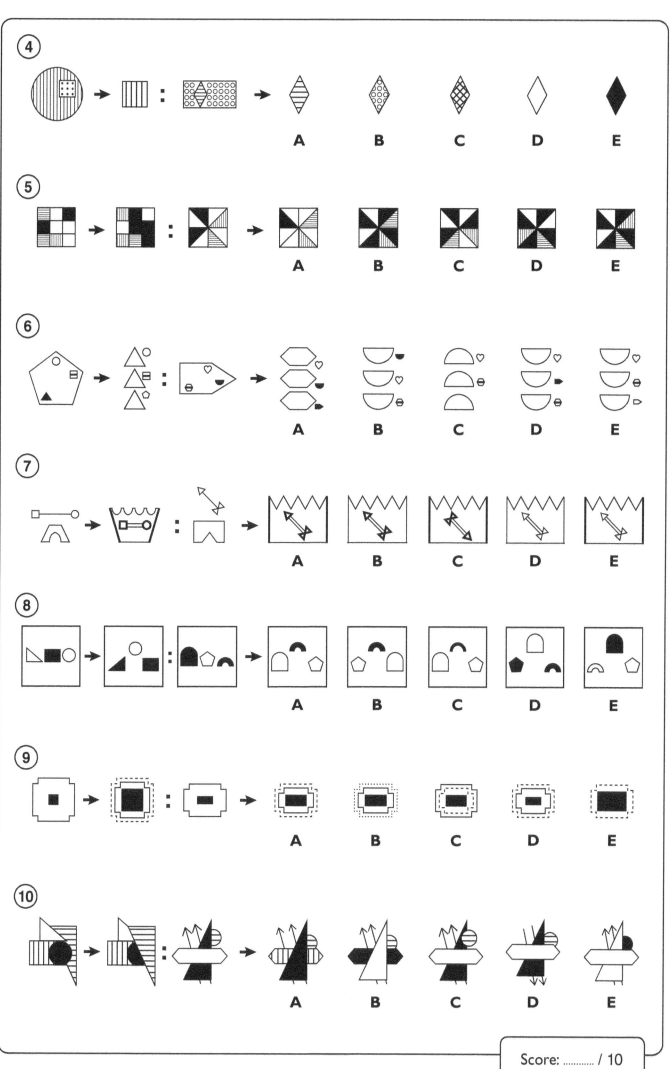

Test 6

You have 5 minutes to complete this test.

You have 10 questions to complete within the given time.

Decide which figure is most unlike the others. Circle the letter below it.

EXAMPLE

Ⓐ   B   C   D   E

①

     A   B   C   D   E

②

     A   B   C   D   E

③

     A   B   C   D   E

Questions continue on next page

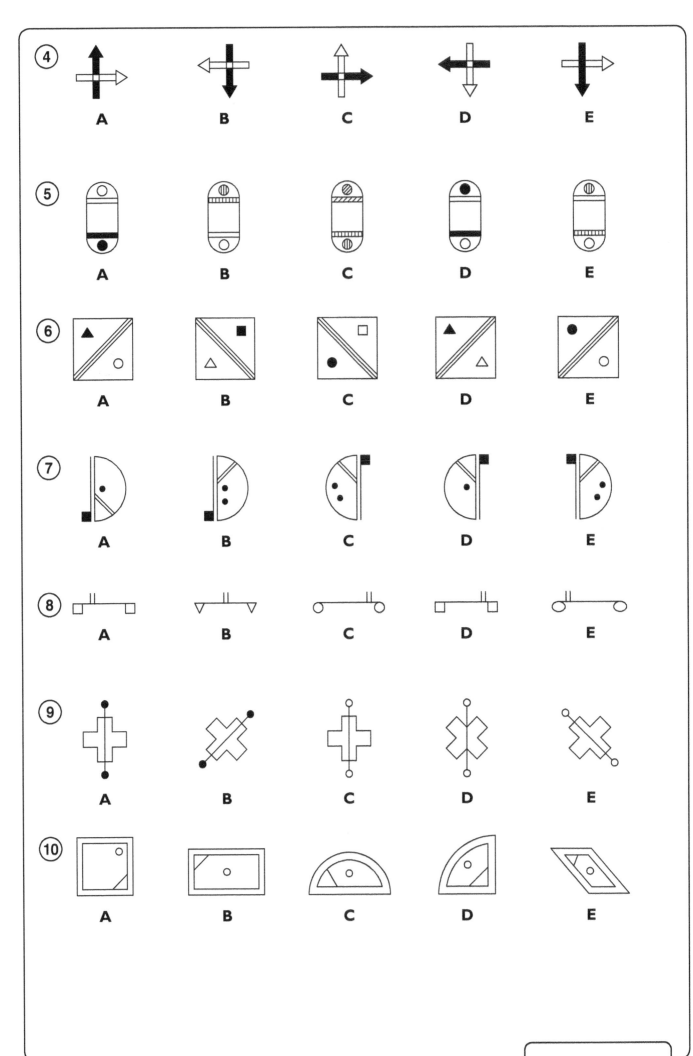

Score: .... / 10

Test 7

You have 5 minutes to complete this test.

You have 10 questions to complete within the given time.

The three figures on the left are similar in some way.

Decide which figure is most similar to the three on the left and circle the letter below it.

A   Ⓑ   C   D   E

①

A   B   C   D   E

②

A   B   C   D   E

③

A   B   C   D   E

Questions continue on next page

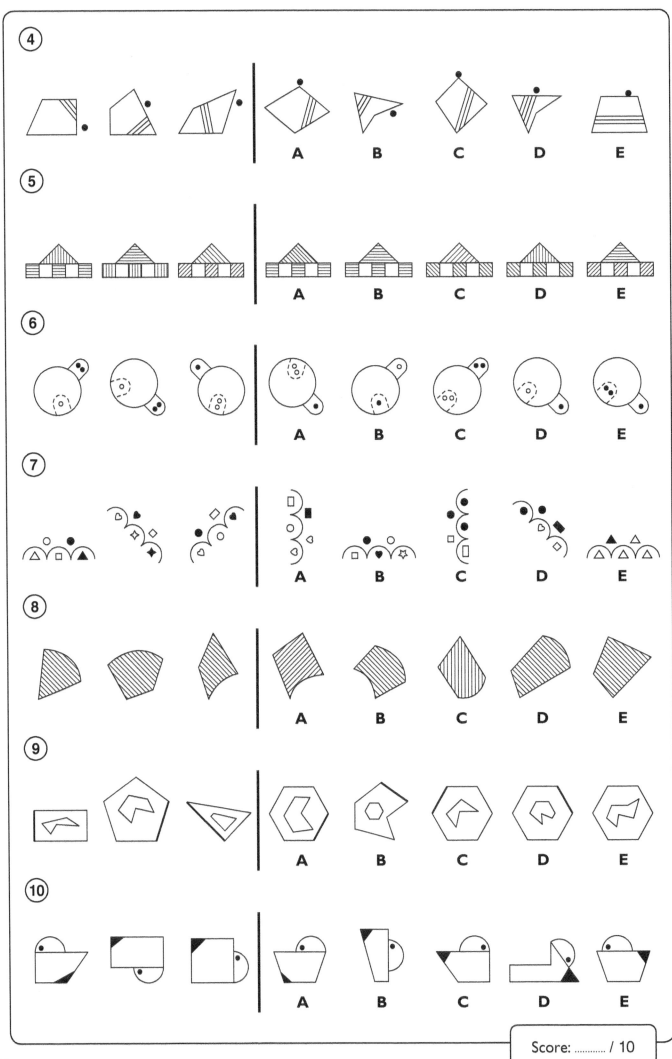

Score: .... / 10

Test 8

You have 5 minutes to complete this test.

You have 10 questions to complete within the given time.

Each figure on the left has a code next to it. Decide how the code letters match the shapes.

Look at the shape on the right and work out its code. Circle the letter below the correct code.

Questions continue on next page

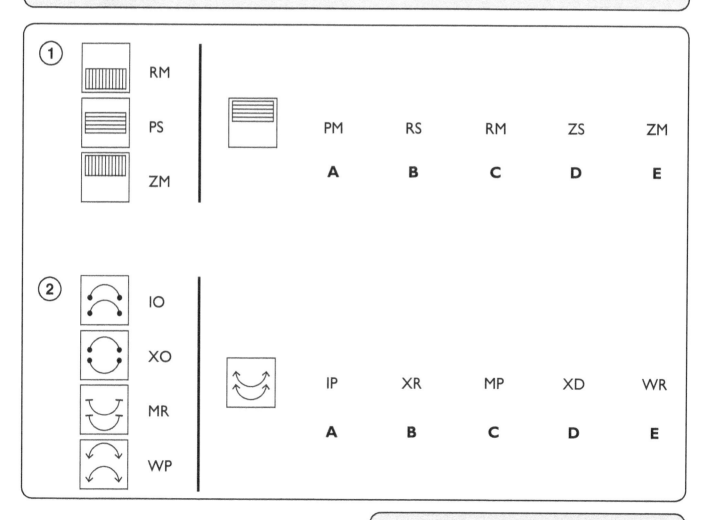

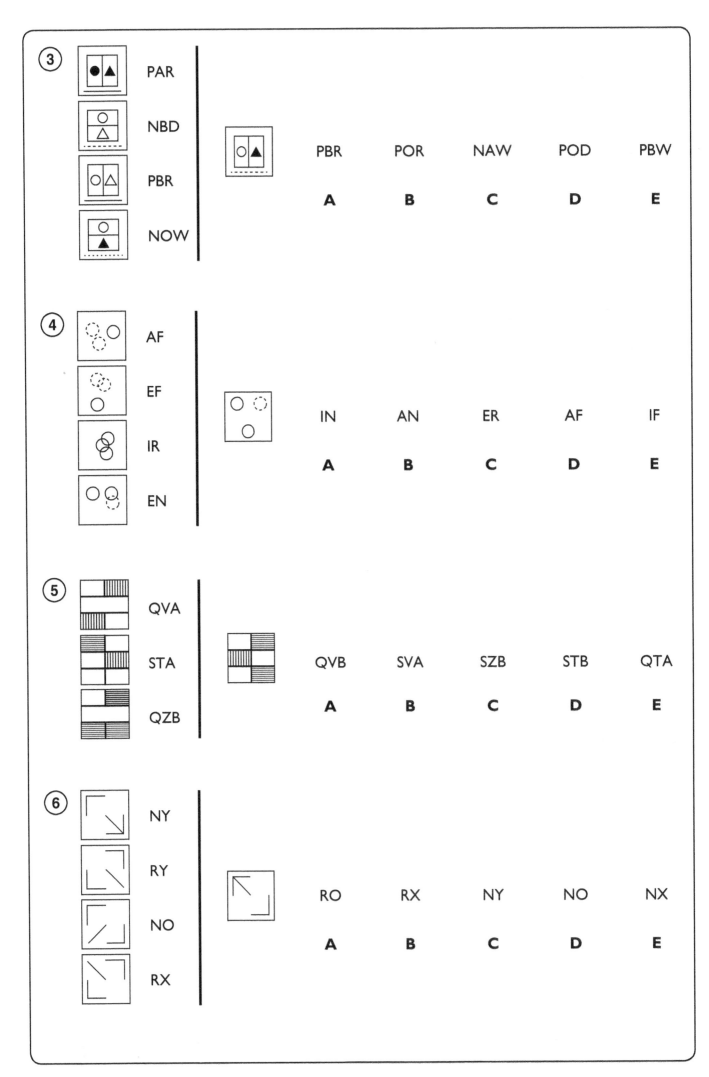

③ PAR · NBD · PBR · NOW

PBR	POR	NAW	POD	PBW
A	**B**	**C**	**D**	**E**

④ AF · EF · IR · EN

IN	AN	ER	AF	IF
A	**B**	**C**	**D**	**E**

⑤ QVA · STA · QZB

QVB	SVA	SZB	STB	QTA
A	**B**	**C**	**D**	**E**

⑥ NY · RY · NO · RX

RO	RX	NY	NO	NX
A	**B**	**C**	**D**	**E**

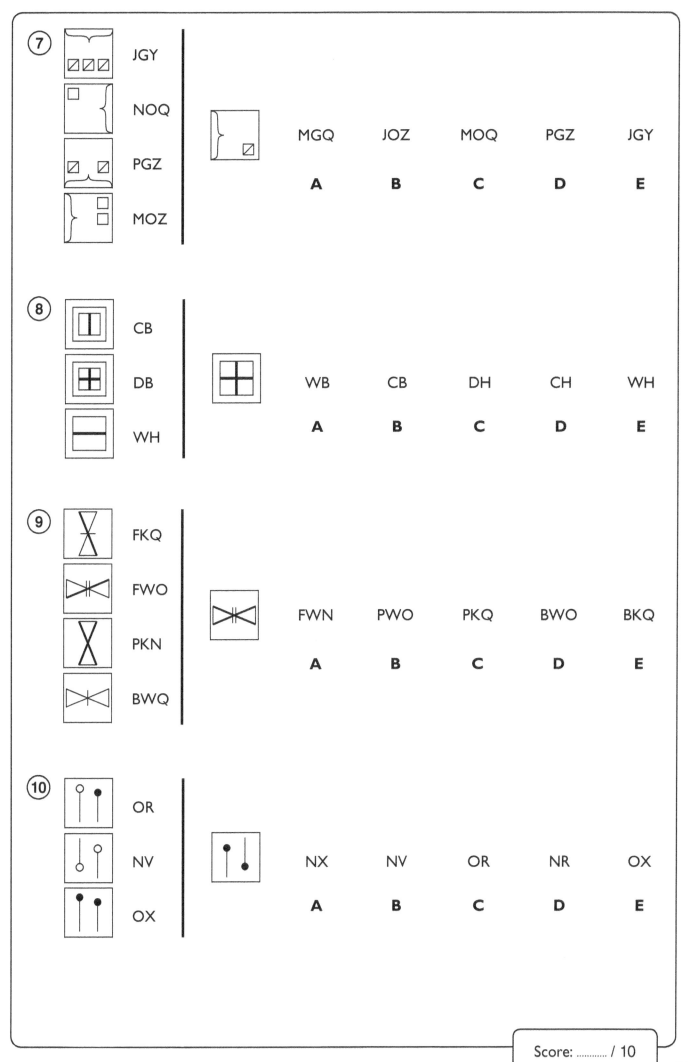

7 | JGY / NOQ / PGZ / MOZ

MGQ	JOZ	MOQ	PGZ	JGY
A	**B**	**C**	**D**	**E**

8 | CB / DB / WH

WB	CB	DH	CH	WH
A	**B**	**C**	**D**	**E**

9 | FKQ / FWO / PKN / BWQ

FWN	PWO	PKQ	BWO	BKQ
A	**B**	**C**	**D**	**E**

10 | OR / NV / OX

NX	NV	OR	NR	OX
A	**B**	**C**	**D**	**E**

Score: .... / 10

Test 9

You have 6 minutes to complete this test.

You have 12 questions to complete within the given time.

The three figures in the oval are similar in some way.

Decide which figure is most similar to the ones in the oval and circle the letter below it.

EXAMPLE

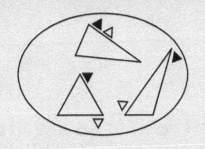

| A | B | C | D | E |

①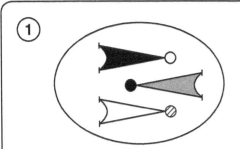

| A | B | C | D | E |

②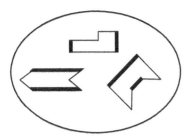

| A | B | C | D | E |

③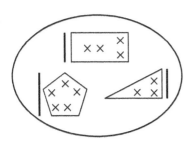

| A | B | C | D | E |

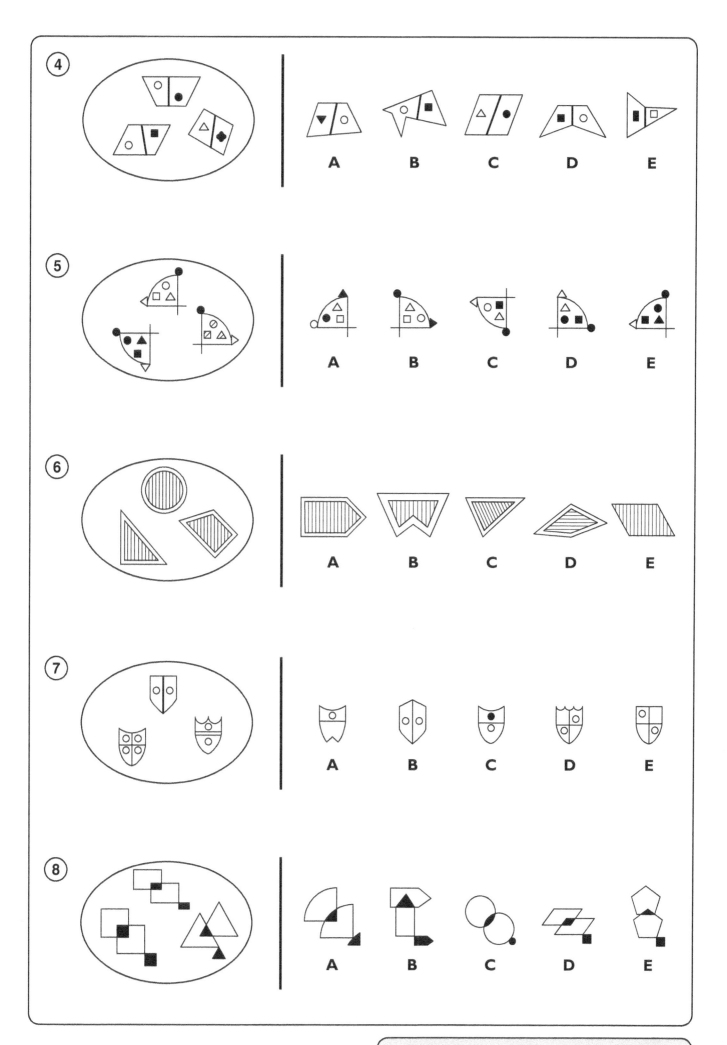

Questions continue on next page

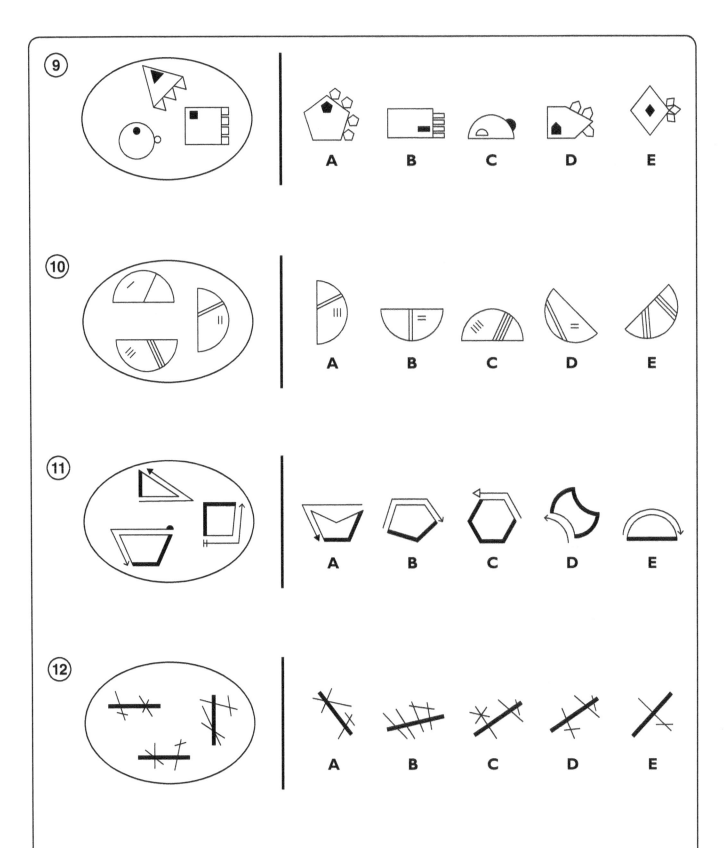

Test 10

You have 6 minutes to complete this test.

You have 12 questions to complete within the given time.

In each question, there is a sequence of triangles with one left empty.

Decide which triangle on the right completes the sequence and circle the letter below it.

EXAMPLE

A   B   C   D   E

---

①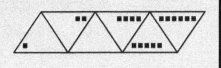

           A   B   C   D   E

②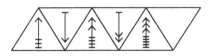

           A   B   C   D   E

③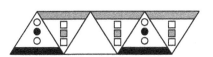

           A   B   C   D   E

④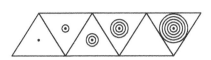

           A   B   C   D   E

Questions continue on next page

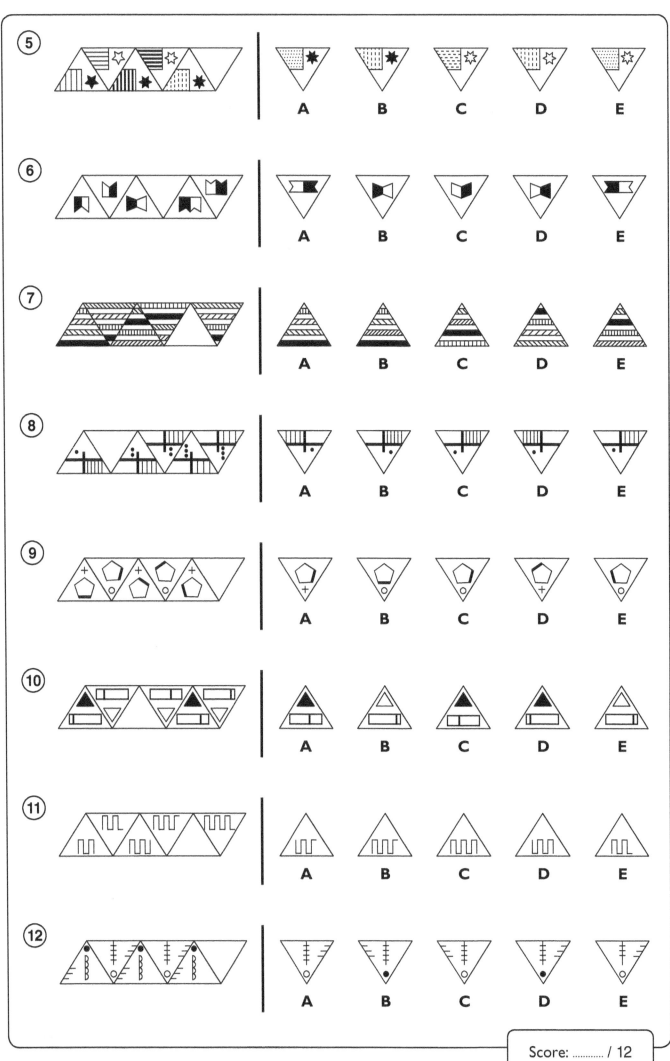

Score: .... / 12

Test 11

You have 6 minutes to complete this test.

You have 12 questions to complete within the given time.

In each star below, one triangle has been left empty.

Decide which triangle completes the star and circle the letter below it.

EXAMPLE

   Ⓐ   B   C   D   E

1

   A   B   C   D   E

2

   A   B   C   D   E

Questions continue on next page

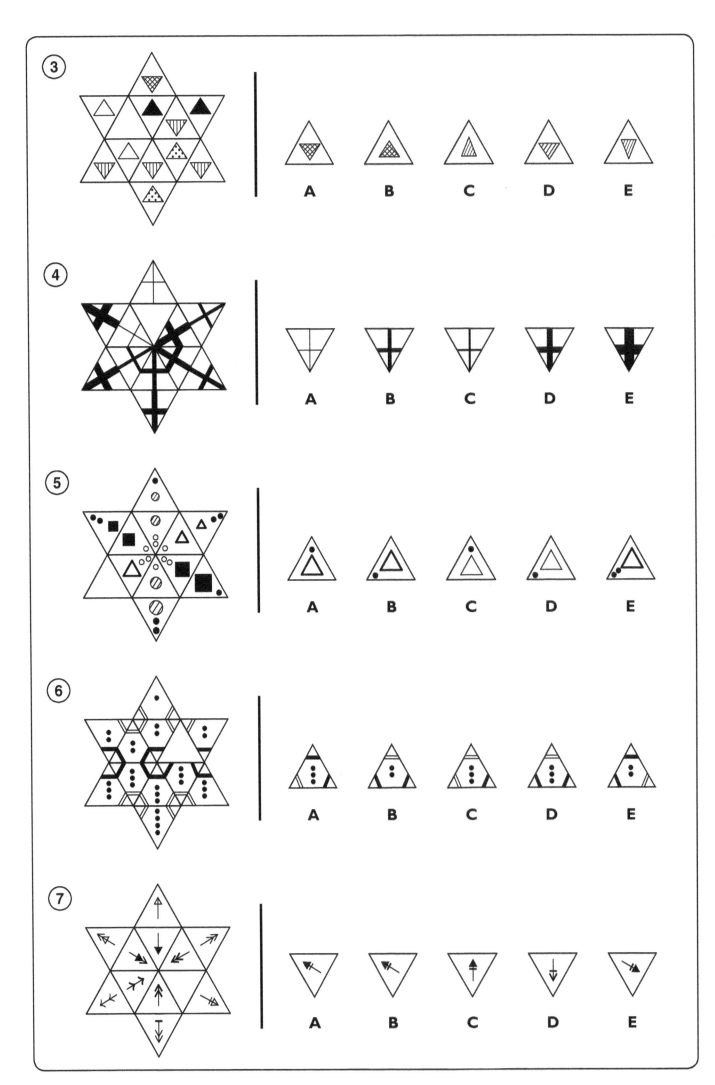

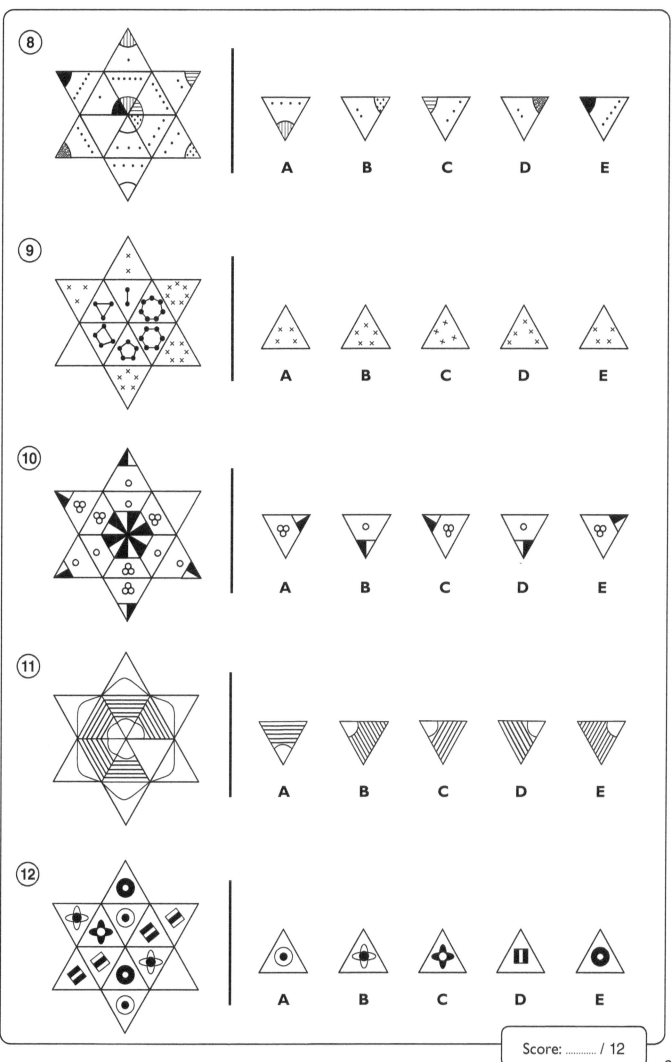

Test 12

You have 6 minutes to complete this test.

You have 12 questions to complete within the given time.

Compare the two large triangles on the left and work out the relationship between them.

Decide which small triangle completes the big triangle and circle the letter below it.

EXAMPLE

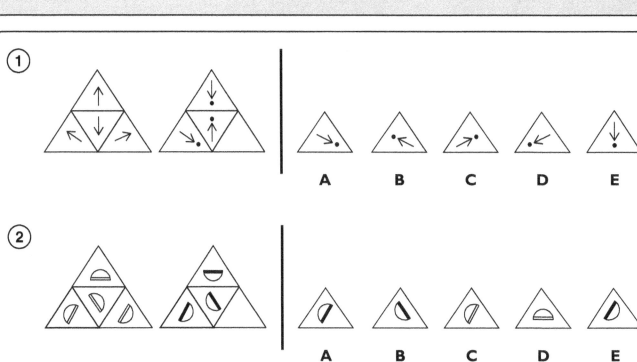

A   B   Ⓒ   D   E

---

①

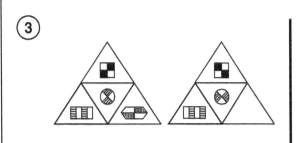

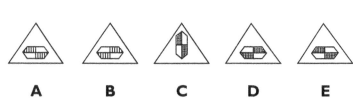

A   B   C   D   E

②

A   B   C   D   E

③

A   B   C   D   E

30

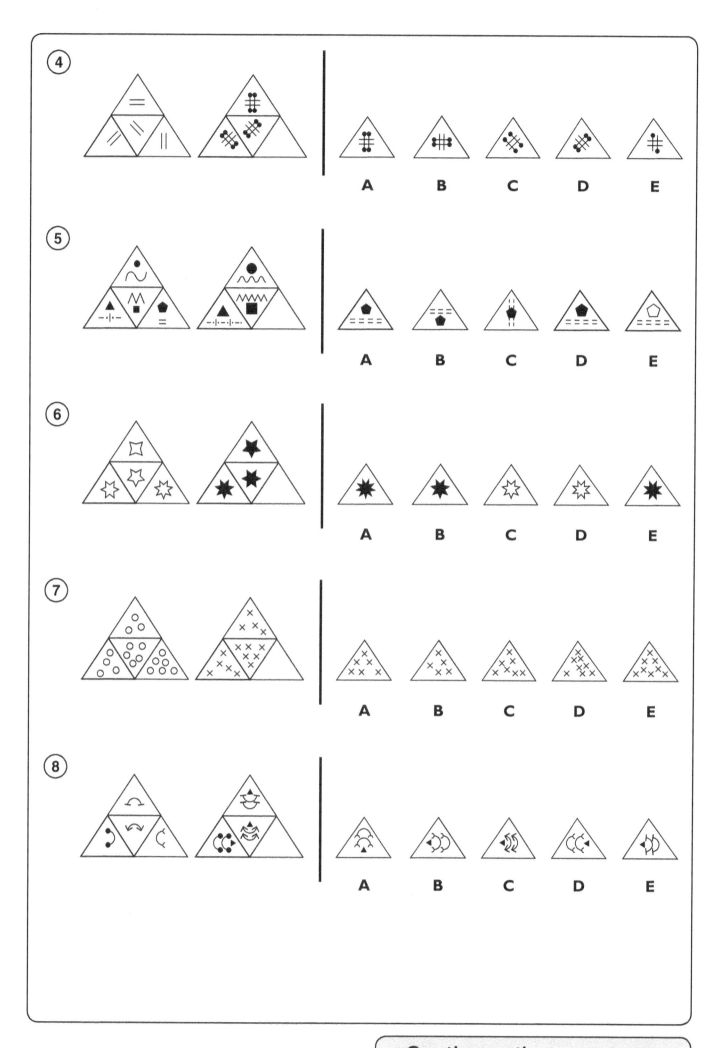

Questions continue on next page

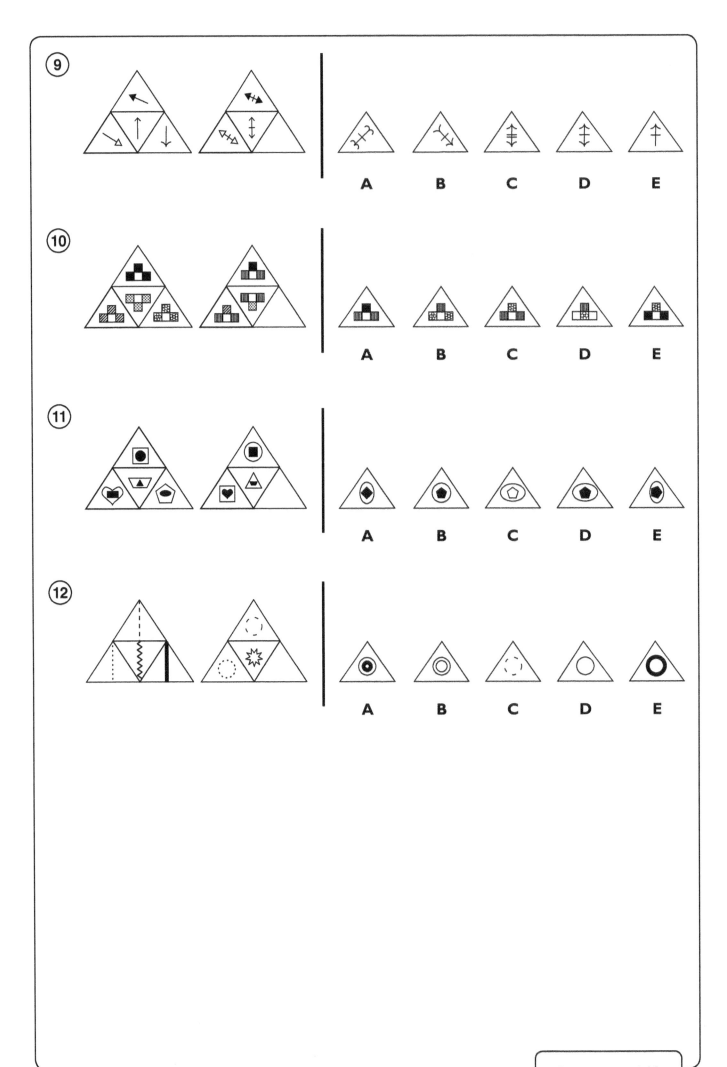

Test 13

There are two figures on the left with an arrow between them. Decide how the second figure is related to the first.

There is then a third figure followed by an arrow and four more figures.

Decide which figure is related to the third in the same way as the first two figures are related. Circle the letter below it.

EXAMPLE

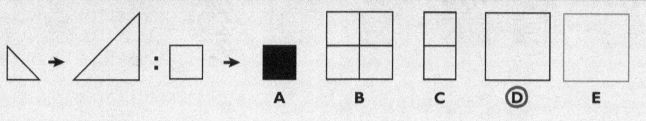

1

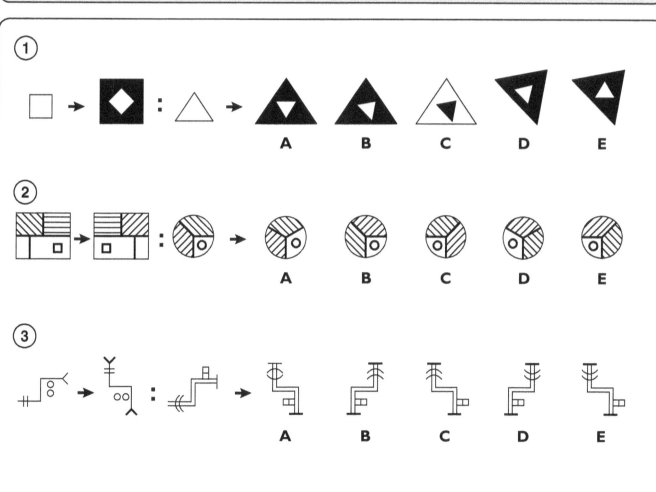

Questions continue on next page

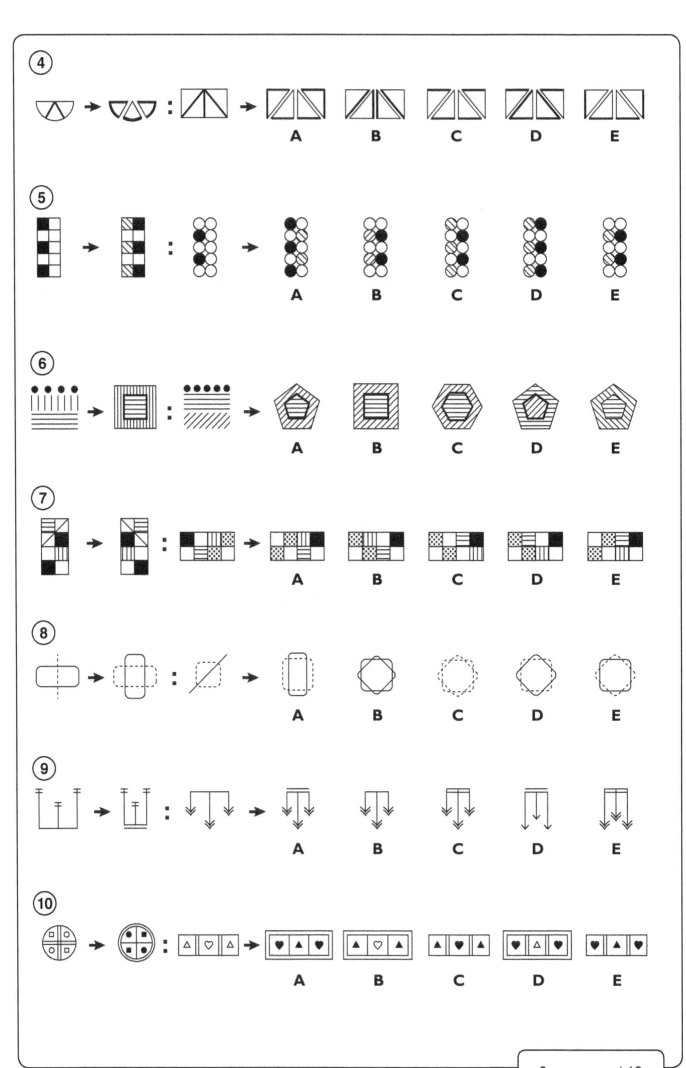

Score: .... / 10

Test 14

You have 6 minutes to complete this test.

You have 12 questions to complete within the given time.

In each grid below, one square has been left empty.

Look at the five squares to the right. Decide which one completes the grid and circle the letter below it.

EXAMPLE

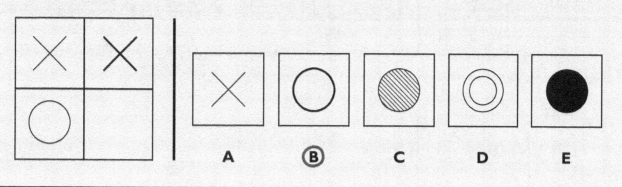

A   Ⓑ   C   D   E

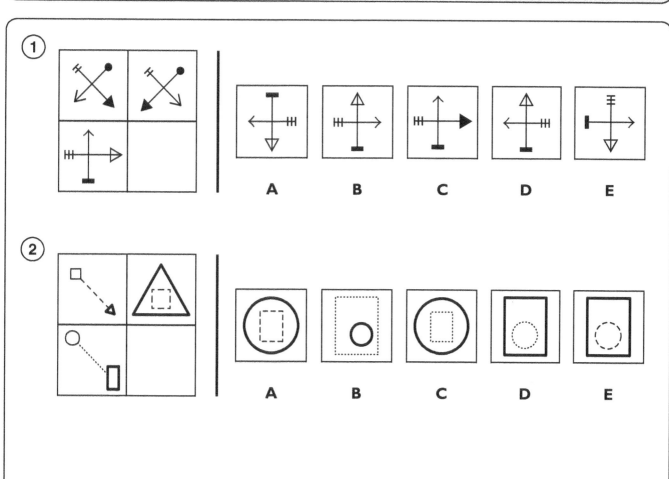

Questions continue on next page

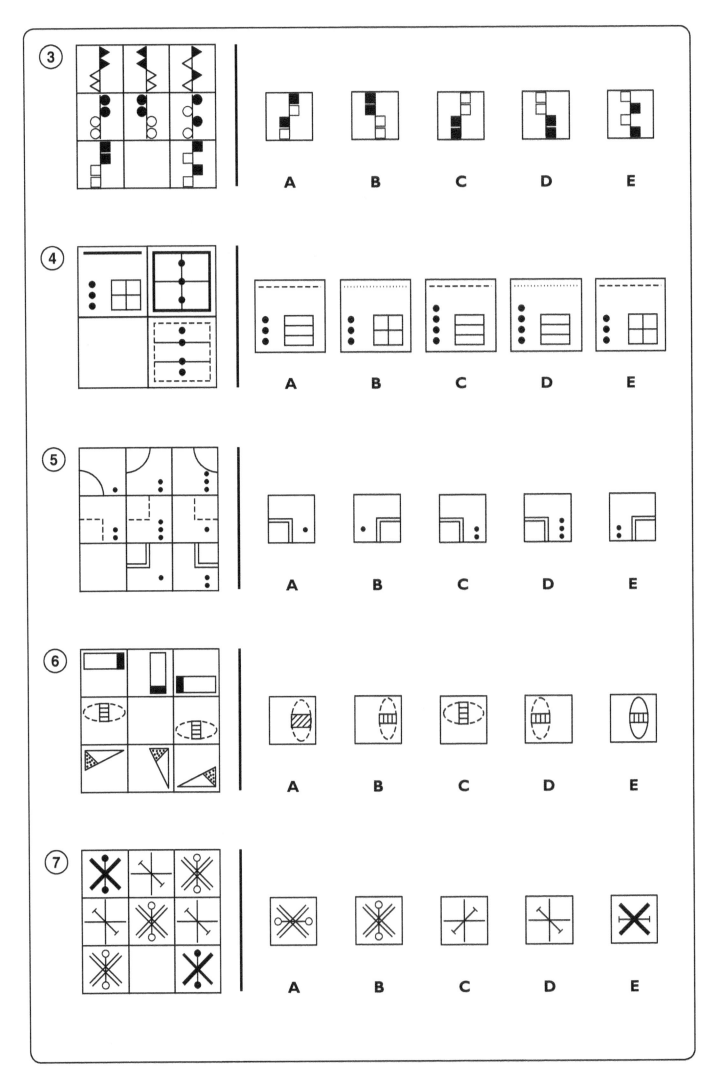

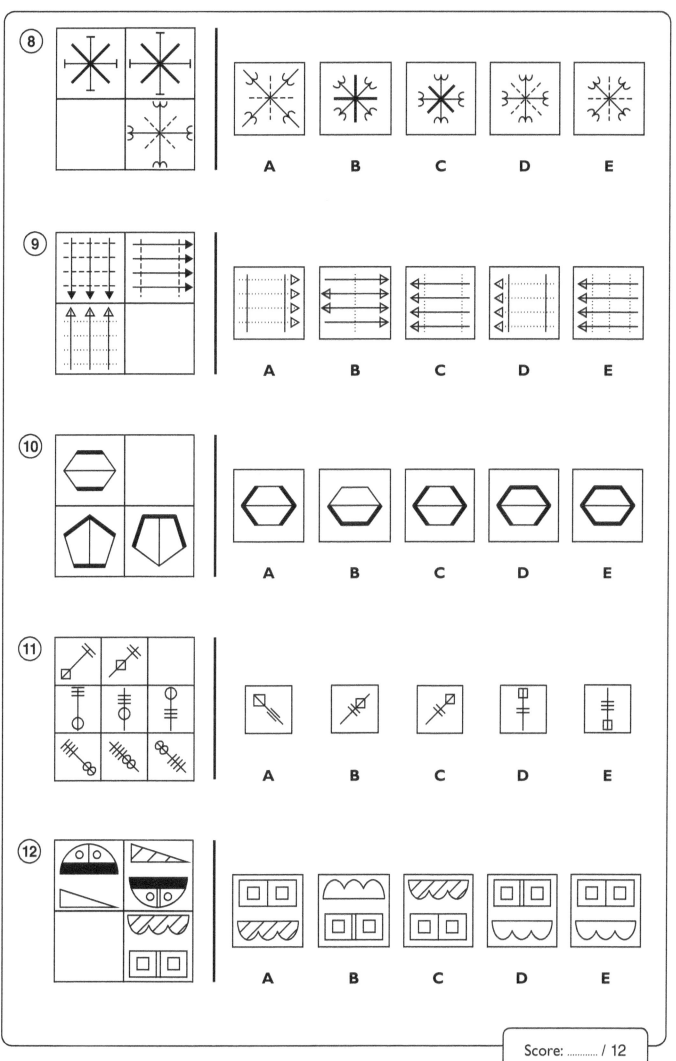

Test 15

You have 5 minutes to complete this test.

You have 10 questions to complete within the given time.

In each question, there is a sequence of squares with one square left empty.

Decide which of the five squares on the right completes the sequence and circle the letter below it.

EXAMPLE

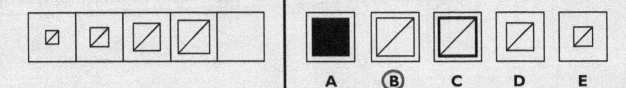

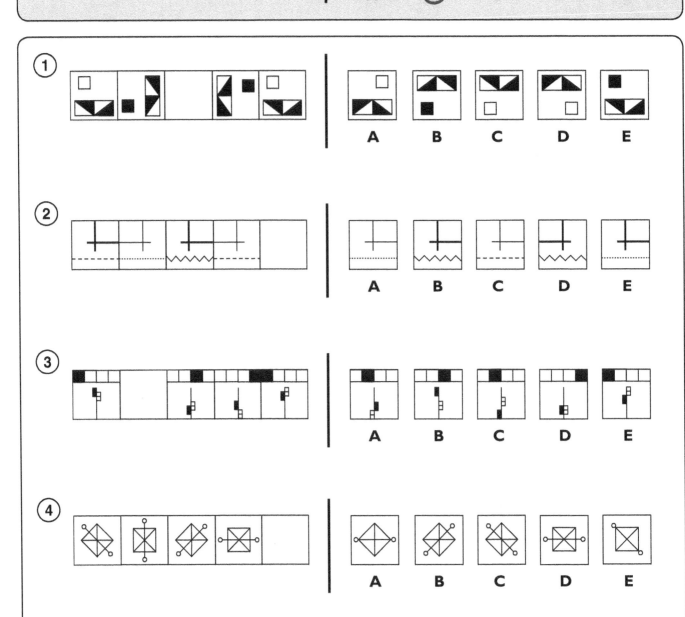

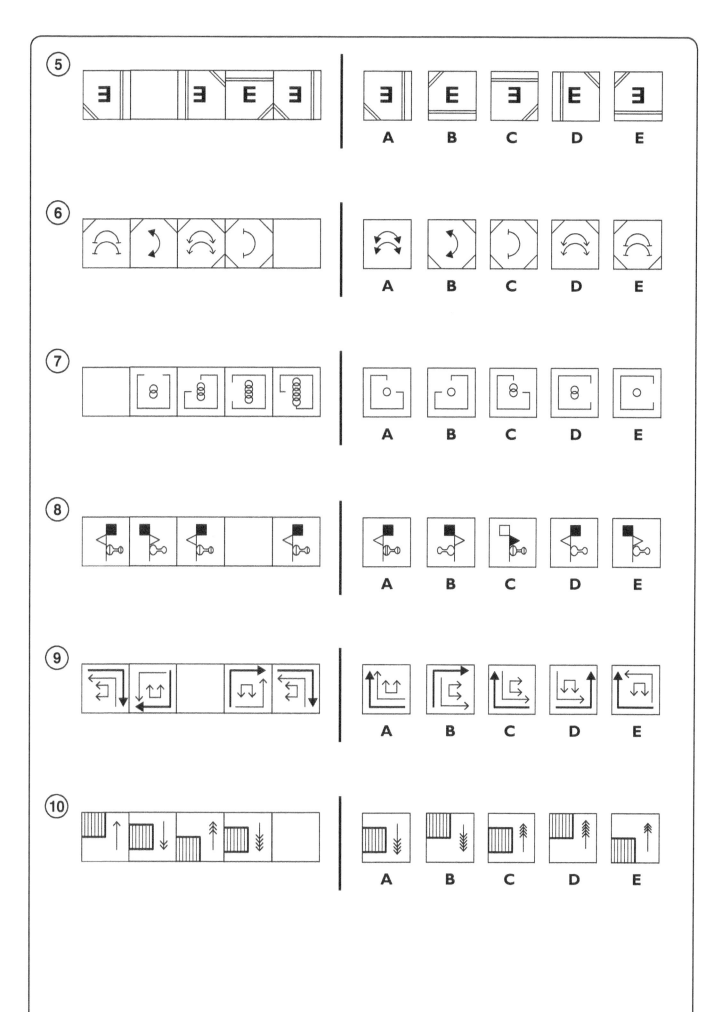

Test 16

You have 5 minutes to complete this test.

You have 10 questions to complete within the given time.

The two figures on the left are similar in some way.

Decide which figure is most similar to the two on the left and circle the letter below it.

EXAMPLE

A   (B)   C   D   E

①

    A   B   C   D   E

②

    A   B   C   D   E

③

    A   B   C   D   E

④

    A   B   C   D   E

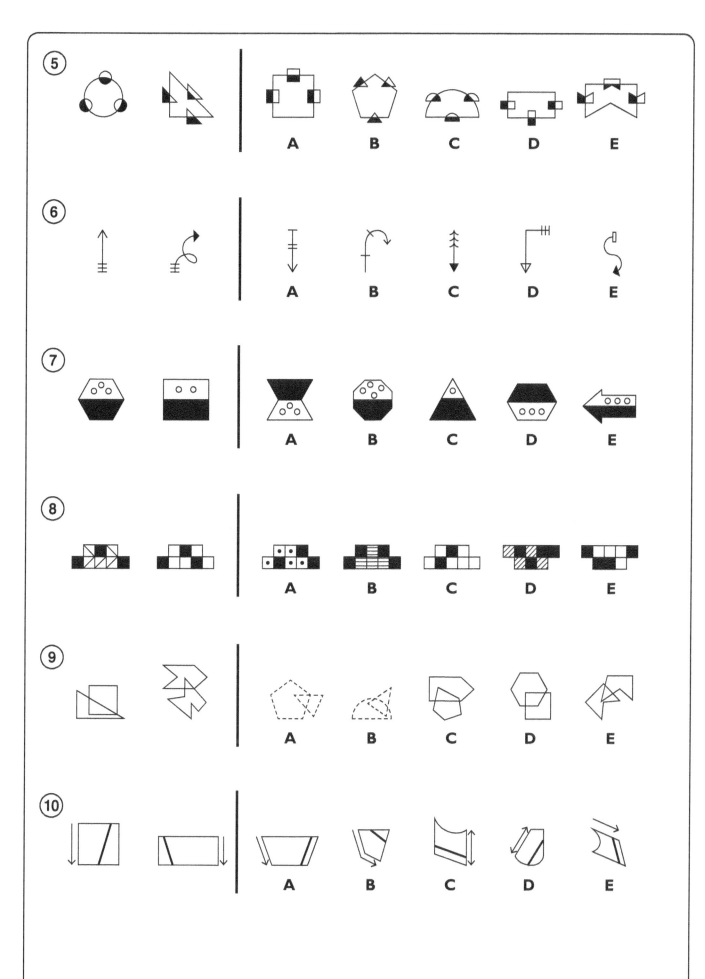

Score: .... / 10

Test 17

You have 5 minutes to complete this test.

You have 10 questions to complete within the given time.

To answer these questions, you have to work out a code.

For the figures on the left, decide how the code letters match the figures. Look at the next figure and work out the missing code. Circle the letter below the correct code.

EXAMPLE

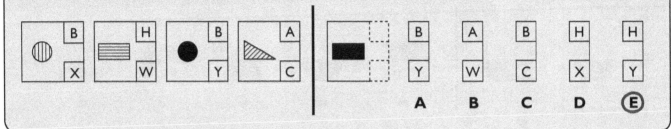

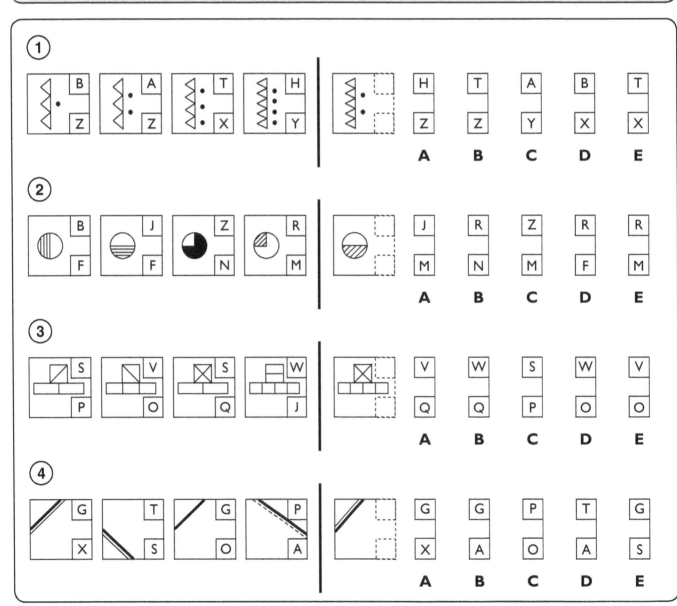

42

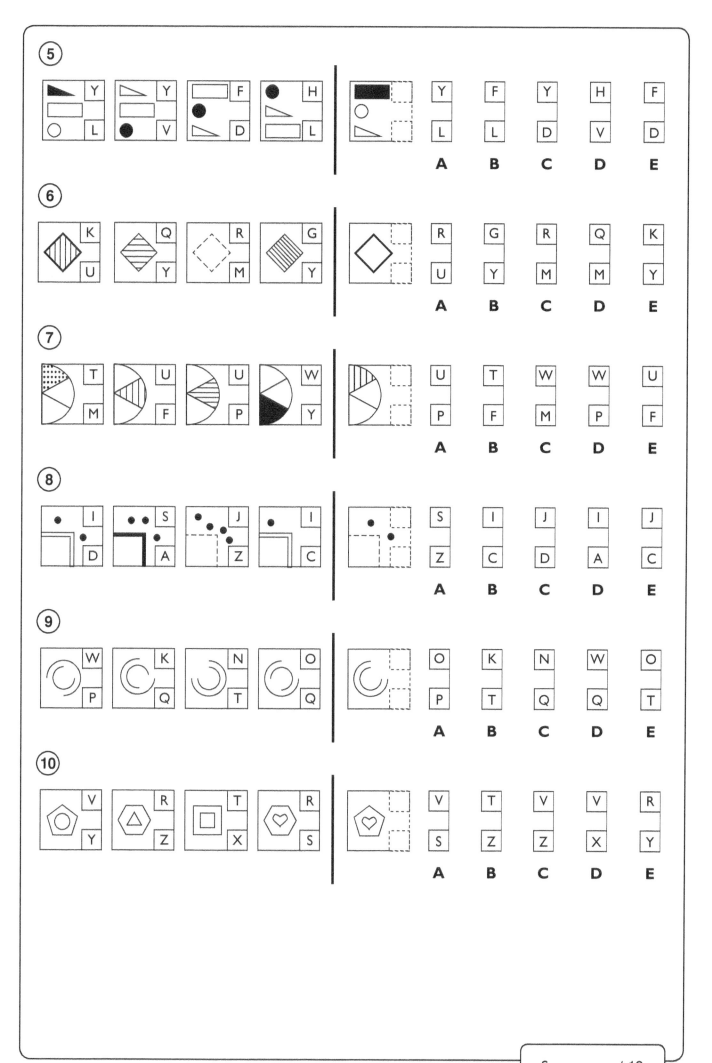

5
A: Y / L
B: F / L
C: Y / D
D: H / V
E: F / D

6
A: R / U
B: G / Y
C: R / M
D: Q / M
E: K / Y

7
A: U / P
B: T / F
C: W / M
D: W / P
E: U / F

8
A: S / Z
B: I / C
C: J / D
D: I / A
E: J / C

9
A: O / P
B: K / T
C: N / Q
D: W / Q
E: O / T

10
A: V / S
B: T / Z
C: V / Z
D: V / X
E: R / Y

Score: .... / 10

43

Test 18

You have 5 minutes to complete this test.

You have 10 questions to complete within the given time.

EXAMPLE

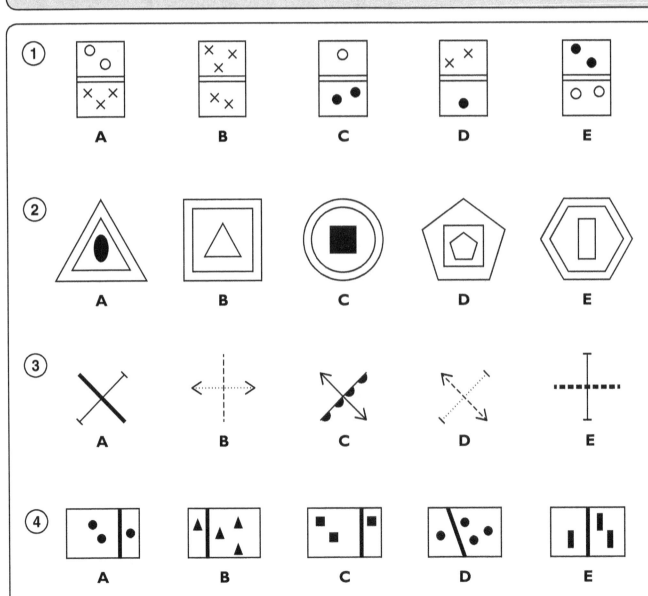

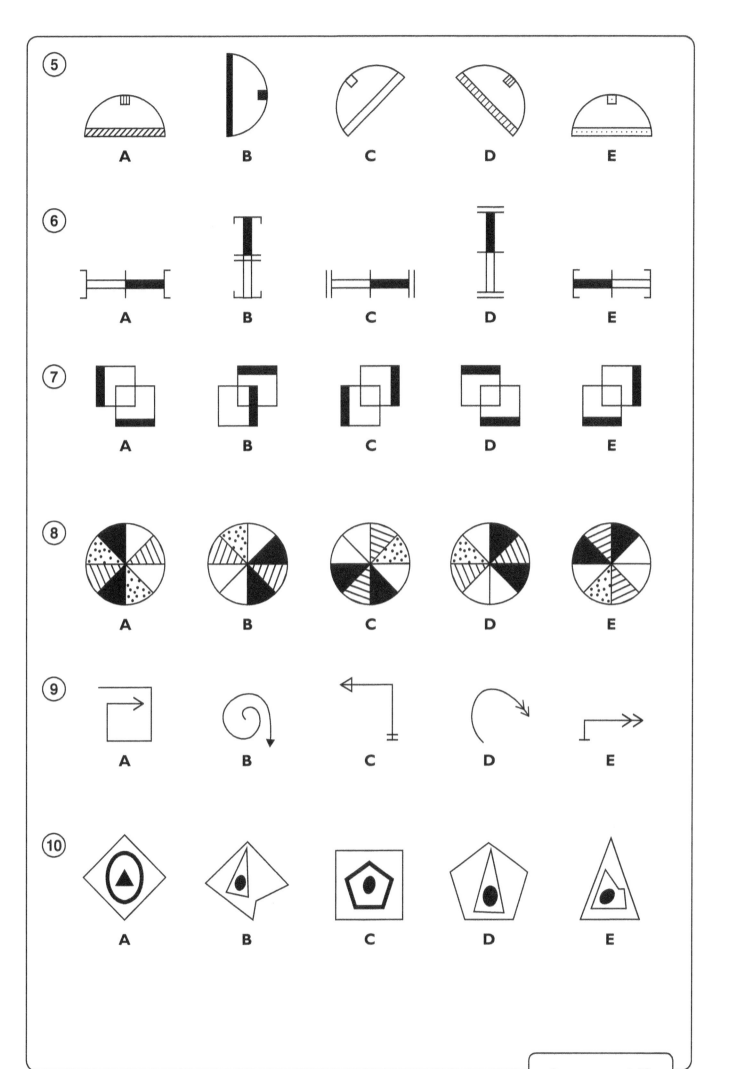

Test 19

You have 5 minutes to complete this test.

You have 10 questions to complete within the given time.

The three figures on the left are similar in some way.

Decide which figure is most similar to the three on the left and circle the letter below it.

EXAMPLE

	A	B	C	D	E

① |

A   B   C   D   E

② |

A   B   C   D   E

③ |

A   B   C   D   E

④ |

A   B   C   D   E

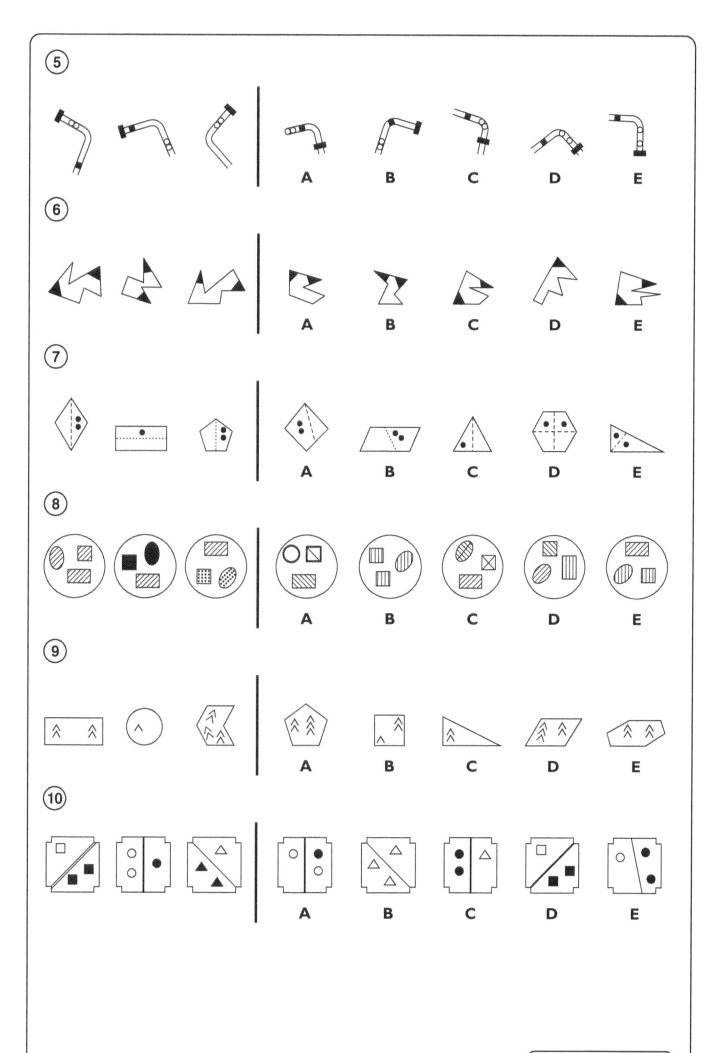

Test 20

You have 5 minutes to complete this test.

You have 10 questions to complete within the given time.

Each figure on the left has a code next to it. Decide how the code letters match the shapes.

Look at the shape on the right and work out its code. Circle the letter below the correct code.

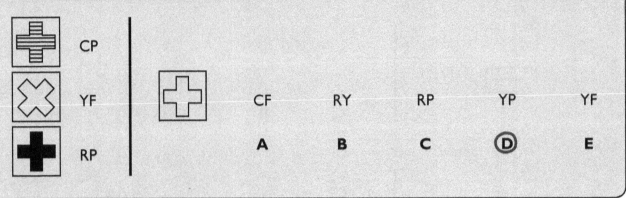

	CF	RY	RP	YP	YF
	A	B	C	D	E

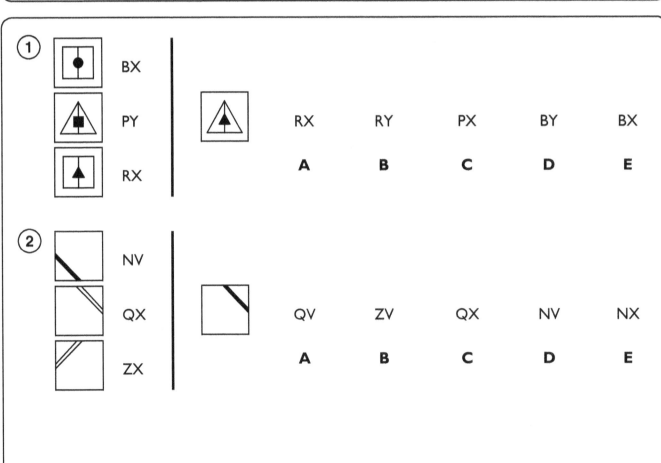

①

	RX	RY	PX	BY	BX
	A	B	C	D	E

②

	QV	ZV	QX	NV	NX
	A	B	C	D	E

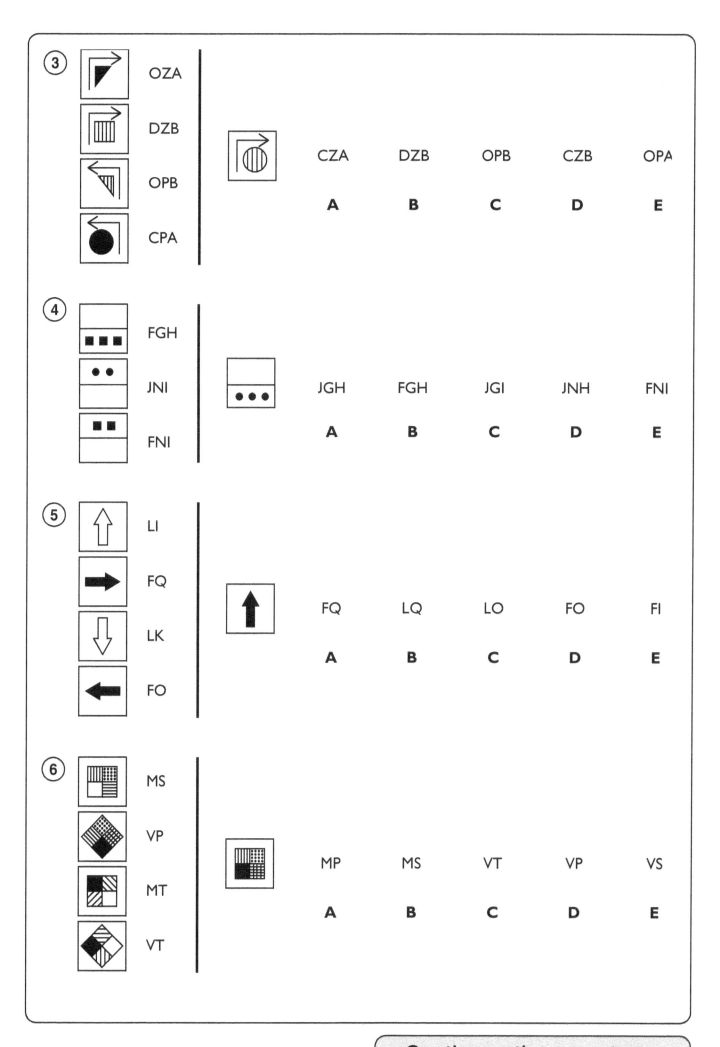

Questions continue on next page

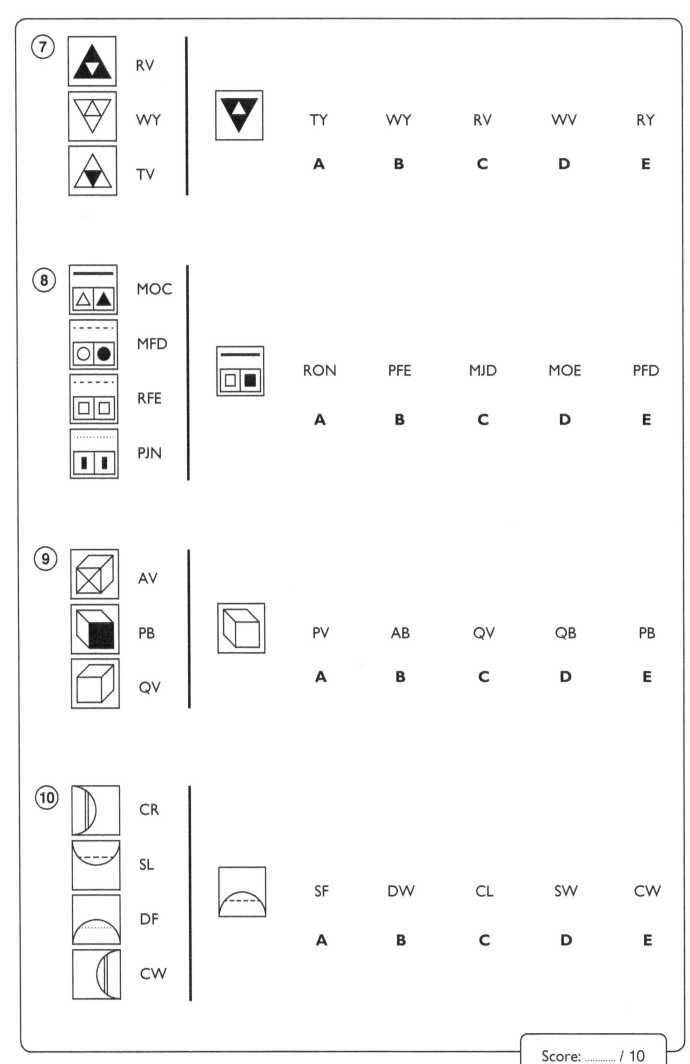

⑦ RV · WY · TV

TY   WY   RV   WV   RY

A   B   C   D   E

⑧ MOC · MFD · RFE · PJN

RON   PFE   MJD   MOE   PFD

A   B   C   D   E

⑨ AV · PB · QV

PV   AB   QV   QB   PB

A   B   C   D   E

⑩ CR · SL · DF · CW

SF   DW   CL   SW   CW

A   B   C   D   E

Score: .... / 10

50

Test 21

You have 6 minutes to complete this test.

You have 12 questions to complete within the given time.

The three figures in the oval are similar in some way.

Decide which figure is most similar to the ones in the oval and circle the letter below it.

EXAMPLE

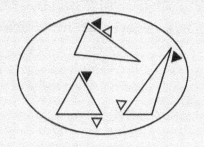

A **(B)** C D E

---

①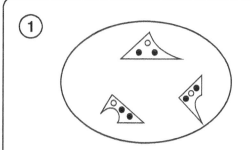

A B C D E

---

②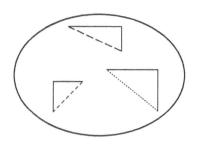

A B C D E

---

③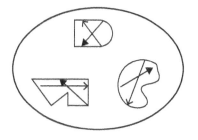

A B C D E

Questions continue on next page

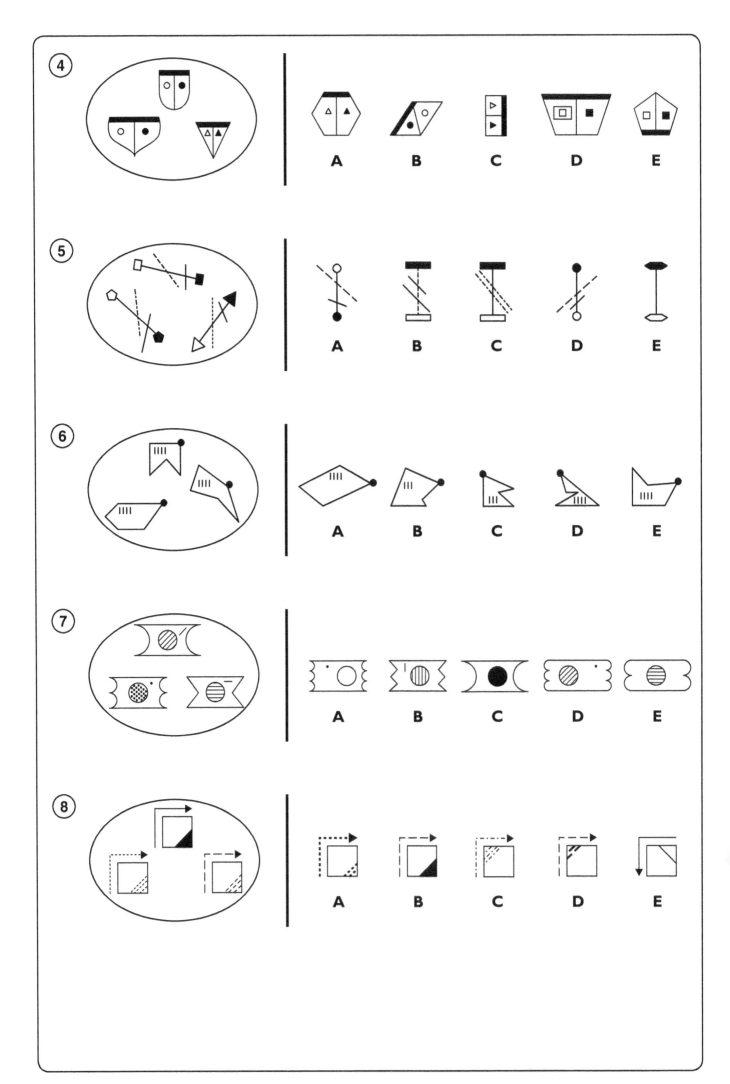

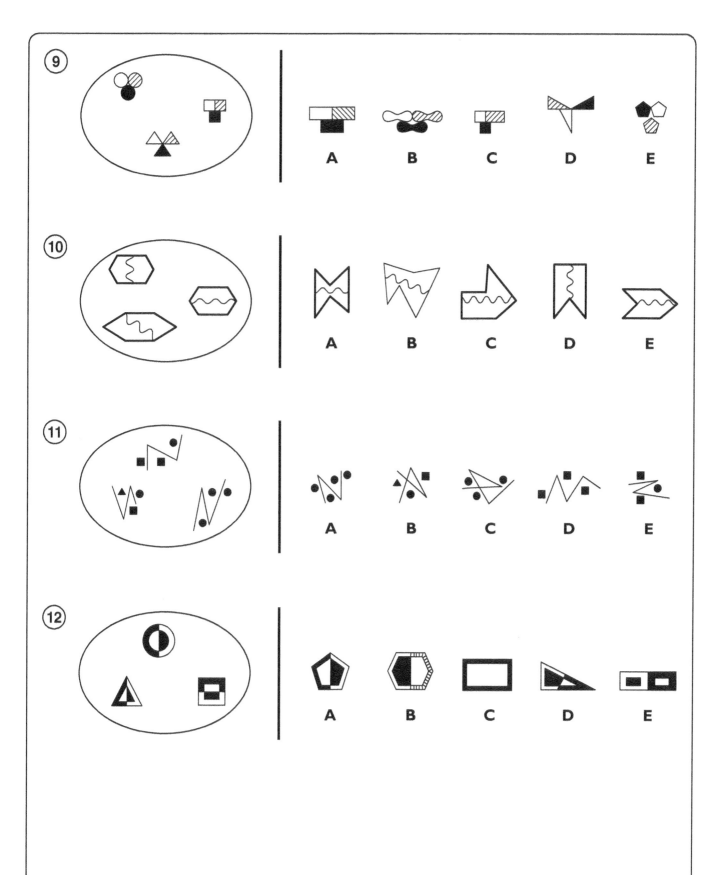

9

A B C D E

10

A B C D E

11

A B C D E

12

A B C D E

Test 22

You have 6 minutes to complete this test.

You have 12 questions to complete within the given time.

In each question, there is a sequence of triangles with one left empty.

Decide which triangle on the right completes the sequence and circle the letter below it.

1

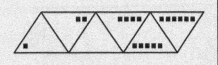

| A | B | C | D | E |

2

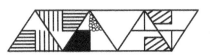

| A | B | C | D | E |

3

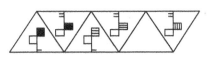

| A | B | C | D | E |

4

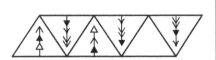

| A | B | C | D | E |

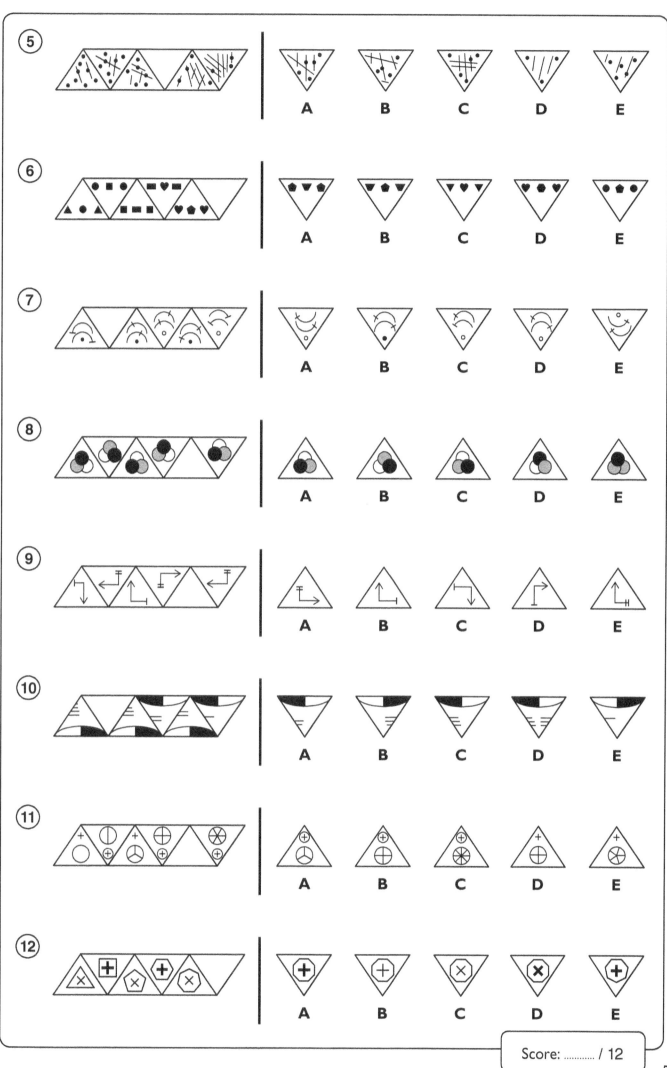

Test 23

You have 6 minutes to complete this test.

You have 12 questions to complete within the given time.

In each star below, one triangle has been left empty.

Decide which triangle completes the star and circle the letter below it.

(A)   B   C   D   E

①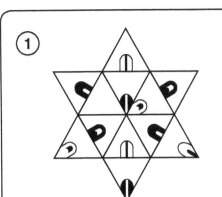

A   B   C   D   E

②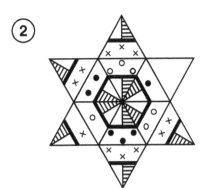

A   B   C   D   E

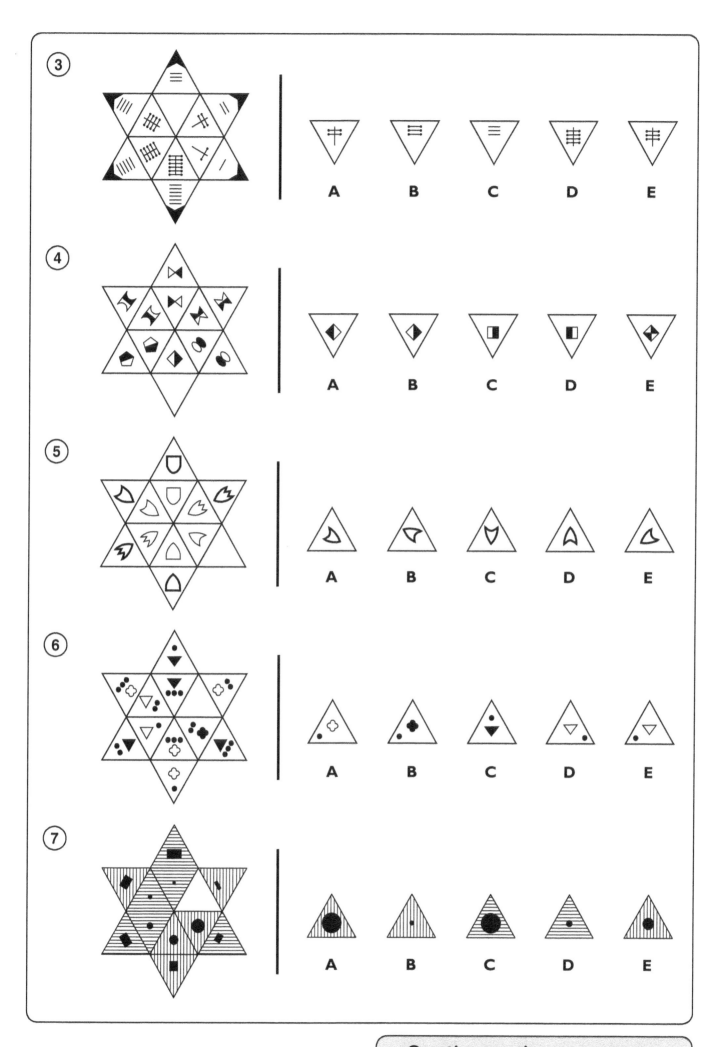

Questions continue on next page

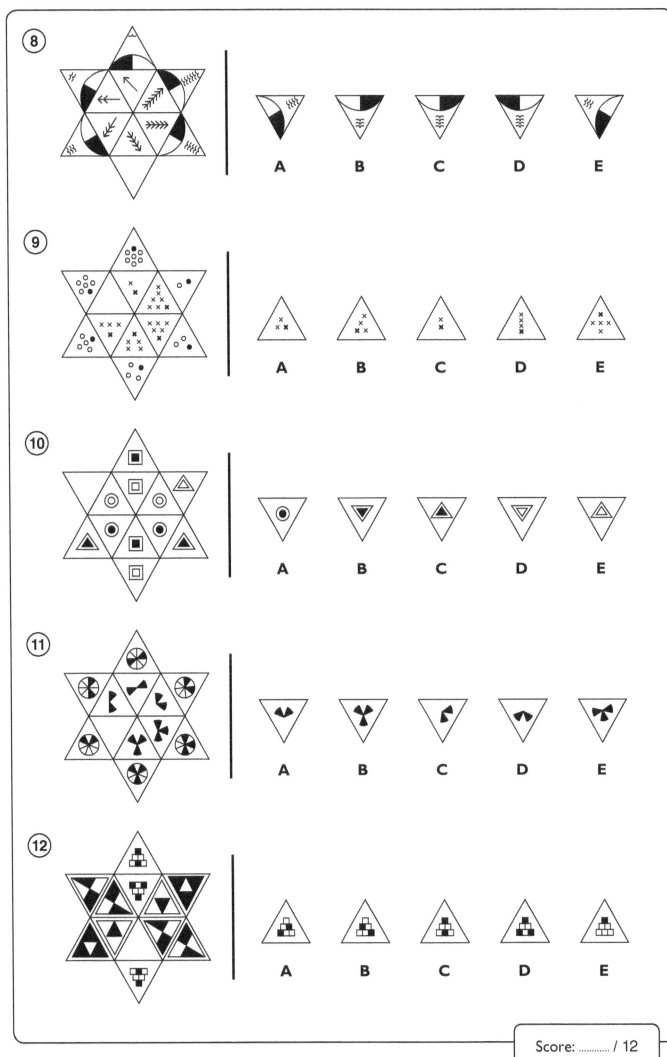

Score: .... / 12

Test 24

You have 6 minutes to complete this test.

You have 12 questions to complete within the given time.

Compare the two large triangles on the left and work out the relationship between them.

Decide which small triangle completes the large triangle and circle the letter below it.

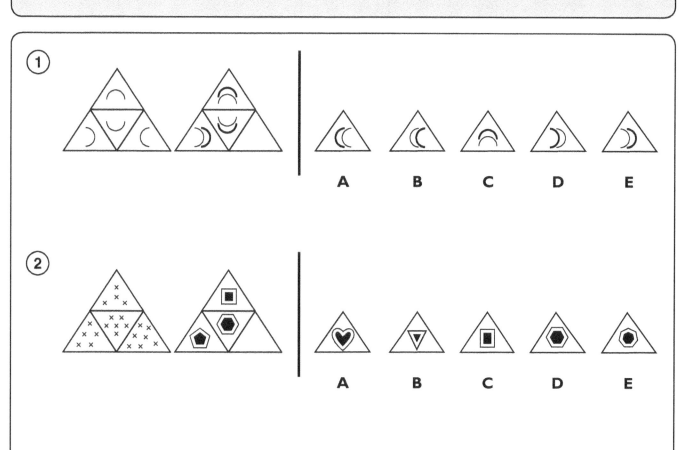

Questions continue on next page

59

Q7   **B**   In each pair of outer and inner triangles, the inner triangle contains the outer triangle's arrow rotated through 180° with the arrowheads and perpendicular lines made bold.

Therefore, the missing triangle should consist of an arrow pointing to the top left corner. It should have a solid triangular arrowhead with a short bold line beneath it.

Therefore, the answer is B.

Q8   **D**   The shading in the corners with an arc is identical within pairs of inner and outer triangles. The number of dots in the outer triangles increases by one each time moving clockwise starting from the top triangle. In the inner triangles, the number of dots decreases by one each time moving clockwise from the top triangle.

Therefore, the missing triangle should consist of a large dotted corner with an arc with two black dots outside.

Therefore, the answer is D.

Q9   **C**   In each outer triangle, the crosses match the positions of the corners of the shape in the inner triangle.

Therefore, the missing triangle should have a trapezium-shaped arrangement of four crosses in the same position and orientation as the corners of the trapezium in the centre.

Therefore, the answer is C.

Q10   **E**   Each outer triangle has a black and then white triangle at the outermost point and the number of white dots alternates between three and one.

Therefore, the missing triangle should consist of a black then white triangle at the outermost point of the triangle, with three touching dots.

Therefore, the answer is E.

Q11   **C**   The inner triangles have corners with an arc that meet to form a flower at the centre of the star. They also have shading which runs parallel to the flat side of the triangle that joins the outer triangle.

Therefore, the missing triangle should consist of a curve-sided triangle in the top left corner with shading running from top right to bottom left.

Therefore, the answer is C.

Q12   **C**   In each line of triangles, from point to point, the shapes alternate in colour.

Therefore, the missing triangle should consist of a black-petalled flower with a white centre.

Therefore, the answer is C.

Test 12

Q1   **D**   Moving from the left to the right triangle, each arrow rotates 180° and a dot appears at the arrowhead.

Therefore, the answer is D.

Q2   **A**   Moving from the left to the right triangle, each semicircle is rotated 180° and the flat side becomes bold.

Therefore, the answer is A.

Q3   **E**   Moving from the left to the right triangle, the shading in each shape is reversed (white parts become shaded). The type of shading does not change.

Therefore, the answer is E.

Q4   **B**   Moving from the left to the right triangle, the parallel lines are combined with another pair of perpendicular parallel lines. The additional lines have a dot at each end.

Therefore, the answer is B.

Q5   **D**   Moving from the left to the right triangle, the black shape is enlarged. The section of line becomes smaller and the pattern frequency is increased to stretch across the widest horizontal part of the triangle.

Therefore, the answer is D.

Q6   **E**   Moving from the left to the right triangle, the stars become black and gain an additional point.

Therefore, the answer is E.

Q7   **C**   Moving from the left to the right triangle, the white dots change to crosses, with one additional cross. The position of the shapes does not remain consistent.

Therefore, the answer is C.

Q8   **B**   Moving from the left to the right triangle, the arcs are rotated 180° and doubled. A black triangle is added in the curve of one arc. The shape at the end of each arc does not change.

Therefore, the answer is B.

Test 12 answers continue on next page

Q9 **D** Moving from the left to the right triangle, a matching arrowhead is added to the opposite end of each arrow and a short perpendicular line is added across the middle.

Therefore, the answer is D.

Q10 **C** Moving from the left to the right triangle, the two outer squares change to vertical stripe shading.

Therefore, the answer is C.

Q11 **D** Moving from the left to the right triangle, the large outer shape reduces, moves to the centre and becomes black. The inner shape enlarges to become the outer shape and becomes white.

Therefore, the answer is D.

Q12 **E** Moving from the left to the right triangle, the vertical line becomes a circle of the same style.

Therefore, the answer is E.

Test 13

Q1 **B** Moving from left to right, the white shape is rotated 45° clockwise and placed inside a matching large black shape of the same orientation as the original white shape.

Therefore, the answer is B.

Q2 **E** Moving from left to right, the shape is reflected in a vertical mirror line.

Therefore, the answer is E.

Q3 **C** Moving from left to right, the figure is rotated 90° clockwise. The shape at the end is made bold and then duplicated on the other end.

Therefore, the answer is C.

Q4 **A** Moving from left to right, the marked sections of the shape are separated so there is a gap between each of them. The bold and fine lines are reversed.

Therefore, the answer is A.

Q5 **E** Moving from left to right, the black shaded sections are changed to diagonal striped sections (slanted from top left to bottom right) and the sections directly beside these are shaded black.

Therefore, the answer is E.

Q6 **D** Moving from left to right, the number of dots gives the number of corners of the shape formed. The upper section of stripes shows the striped shading for the outer shape and

the lower section of stripes shows the striped shading of the inner shape. The inner shape has a bold line around it.

Therefore, the answer is D.

Q7 **B** Moving from left to right, the shape is reflected in a vertical mirror line.

Therefore, the answer is B.

Q8 **E** Moving from left to right, the line bisecting the shape is replaced by a duplicate shape. The bisecting line in the left-hand figure shows the style of outline for the original shape in the right-hand figure and the orientation of the second shape.

Therefore, the answer is E.

Q9 **A** Moving from left to right, the vertical lines move closer together and the long horizontal line is doubled.

Therefore, the answer is A.

Q10 **A** Moving from left to right, the small white circles and squares switch places and turn black. The inner double and outer single lines also change places.

Therefore, the answer is A.

Test 14

Q1 **B** Moving from left to right, the arrowheads swap.

Therefore, the answer is B.

Q2 **D** Moving from left to right, the bold shape enlarges and the fine-lined shape moves inside it. The connecting line in the left-hand figure shows the outline style for the inner shape in the right-hand figure.

Therefore, the answer is D.

Q3 **B** In each row, the first two figures are mirror images of one another.

Therefore, the answer is B.

Q4 **C** Moving from left to right, the shape in the bottom right corner enlarges and the line at the top gives the style for its outline. The black dots move to the centre.

Therefore, the answer is C.

Q5 **D** In each row and column there are one, two and three dots. The shape is in the same position in each square in a column.

Therefore, the answer is D.

Q6 B In each row, the figure rotates 90° clockwise each time. The figures lie on the right-hand side of the box in the second column.

Therefore, the answer is B.

Q7 D The figures in each diagonal row running from top right to bottom left are identical.

Therefore, the answer is D.

Q8 D Moving from left to right, the vertical and horizontal lines elongate. The diagonal cross does not alter.

Therefore, the answer is D.

Q9 C Moving from left to right, the figure rotates 90° anticlockwise. The arrows increase in number by one. The middle two dashed or dotted lines disappear.

Therefore, the answer is C.

Q10 D Moving from left to right, the shape rotates 180°. The uppermost horizontal line remains bold but the other bold and fine lines are reversed.

Therefore, the answer is D.

Q11 C Moving from left to right along each row, the small shape moves upwards along the line and the perpendicular lines move downwards.

Therefore, the answer is C.

Q12 E Moving from left to right, the upper shape rotates 180° and the vertical line doubles. The lower shape moves upwards and a diagonal stripe is added (from top right to bottom left).

Therefore, the answer is E.

Test 15

Q1 D Moving from left to right, the figure rotates 90° anticlockwise each time. The small square alternates between being black and white.

Therefore, the missing figure should have the rectangle at the top of the square (with the top left and bottom right triangles shaded). The small square should be white and in the bottom right-hand corner.

Therefore, the answer is D.

Q2 E Moving from left to right, the crossing lines alternate between bold and fine each time. The position of the lines alternates between left and right. The horizontal line follows the sequence: dashes, dots, zigzags.

Therefore, the missing figure should consist of bold crossing lines in the top right corner with a dotted horizontal line.

Therefore, the answer is E.

Q3 C Moving from left to right, the black square at the top moves one place to the right each time. The black rectangle moves upwards until it gets to the top and starts at the bottom again. The white double square moves downwards until it gets to the bottom and starts at the top again.

Therefore, in the missing figure, the second square from the left should be black. There should be a black rectangle on the bottom left of the vertical line and a white double square on the right just below the top of the line.

Therefore, the answer is C.

Q4 C Moving from left to right, the square rotates 45° clockwise in each figure.

Therefore, the missing figure should consist of a diagonally positioned square with the line through the middle running from top left to bottom right.

Therefore, the answer is C.

Q5 B Moving from left to right, the E shape is reflected in adjacent figures. The double horizontal and diagonal lines rotate 90° clockwise each time.

Therefore, the missing figure should contain a forward-facing E shape. The double horizontal line should be at the base of the figure and the double diagonal line should be in the top left-hand corner.

Therefore, the answer is B.

Q6 A Moving from left to right, the figures alternate between double arcs with the open side downwards and single arcs with the open side to the left. The ends of the arcs alternate between perpendicular lines, black triangles and arrowheads. The diagonal lines in the corners increase by one and after all four corners are filled, the sequence begins again from zero.

Therefore, the missing figure should consist of a double arc with black triangles at the ends and three diagonal lines in the corners.

Therefore, the answer is A.

Test 15 answers continue on next page

Q7 A Moving from left to right, the gap in the square moves 45° anticlockwise each time and the number of white overlapping circles increases by one.

Therefore, the missing figure should contain a square with a gap in the top right-hand corner and a single circle.

Therefore, the answer is A.

Q8 E Moving from left to right, the figures alternate so that every other one is the same.

Therefore, the missing figure should contain a vertical line with a black square on the top left and a white triangle with an irregular white vase shape below it on the right.

Therefore, the answer is E.

Q9 C Moving from left to right, the bold arrow and double-headed arrow rotate 90° clockwise. The fine arrow rotates 90° anticlockwise.

Therefore, the missing figure should contain a bold arrow running along the bottom and up the left-hand side, a fine arrow running down the left-hand side and along the bottom and a double-headed arrow pointing right.

Therefore, the answer is C.

Q10 D Moving from left to right, the square moves down and then upwards. The arrowheads increase by one each time and the direction of the arrow alternates between up and down.

Therefore, the missing figure should contain a vertically striped square in the top left-hand corner and five arrowheads on an upward-pointing arrow.

Therefore, the answer is D.

Test 16

Q1 C Each figure on the left consists of concentric shapes. The number of dots is the same as the number of concentric shapes and the number of short vertical lines is the same as the number of vertices.

Therefore, the answer is C.

Q2 D Each figure on the left consists of a double-lined irregular pentagon, with a black circle on one corner and an arrow pointing to another corner.

Therefore, the answer is D.

Q3 A Each figure on the left consists of a circle divided into sectors. The number of scallops outside the circle matches the number of sectors inside the circle. The lower shaded sector has horizontal stripes and the upper one has vertical stripes. All the stripes have identical spacing.

Therefore, the answer is A.

Q4 E Each figure on the left consists of a diagonally striped shape (from top right to bottom left), with a white shape in front of it, which is divided into halves by a bold line.

Therefore, the answer is E.

Q5 D Each figure on the left consists of a white shape with three matching smaller shapes overlapping the edge. One of the overlapping shapes is shaded black inside the larger shape and two are shaded black outside the larger shape.

Therefore, the answer is D.

Q6 D Each figure on the left consists of an arrow with three parallel lines at the end.

Therefore, the answer is D.

Q7 B Each figure on the left consists of a shape divided in half. The lower half is shaded black and the upper half contains small white dots. The number of dots is half the number of sides of the shape.

Therefore, the answer is B.

Q8 A Each figure on the left consists of eight small squares. Three are shaded black.

Therefore, the answer is A.

Q9 B Each figure on the left consists of two overlapping shapes. One shape has one more side than the other.

Therefore, the answer is B.

Q10 A Each figure on the left consists of a quadrilateral with a straight parallel single-headed arrow outside it and a bold diagonal line inside it.

Therefore, the answer is A.

Test 17

Q1 C The upper letter signifies the number of dots. The lower letter signifies the number of triangles.

B = one dot
A = two dots
T = three dots
H = four dots
Z = three triangles

X = four triangles
Y = five triangles

Therefore, the code is AY.

Q2 D The upper letter signifies the type of shading.
The lower letter signifies the fraction of the
circle that is shaded.

B = vertical shading
J = horizontal shading
Z = black shading
R = diagonal shading
F = half shaded
N = three quarters shaded
M = one quarter shaded

Therefore, the code is RF.

Q3 B The upper letter signifies the number of
rectangles. The lower letter signifies the
direction of the lines in the upper square.

S = two rectangles
V = three rectangles
W = four rectangles
P = diagonal line, top right to bottom left
O = diagonal line, top left to bottom right
Q = cross
J = horizontal line

Therefore, the code is WQ.

Q4 E The upper letter signifies the position of the
diagonal corner line. The lower letter signifies
the style of line.

G = top left corner
T = bottom left corner
P = top right corner
X = bold line outside fine line
S = fine line outside bold line
O = single bold line
A = dashed line inside bold line

Therefore, the code is GS.

Q5 B The upper letter signifies the order of shapes
from top to bottom. The lower letter signifies
the position of the black shape.

Y = triangle, rectangle, circle
F = rectangle, circle, triangle
H = circle, triangle, rectangle
L = top shape black
V = bottom shape black
D = middle shape black

Therefore, the code is FL.

Q6 A The upper letter signifies the shading of the
square. The lower letter signifies the outline of
the square.

K = vertical stripe shading
Q = horizontal stripe shading
R = no shading
G = diagonal stripe shading
U = bold outline
Y = fine outline
M = dashed outline

Therefore, the code is RU.

Q7 B The upper letter signifies which sector has been
shaded. The lower letter signifies the shading.

T = upper sector shaded
U = middle sector shaded
W = lower sector shaded
M = dotted shading
F = vertical stripe shading
P = horizontal stripe shading
Y = black shading

Therefore, the code is TF.

Q8 C The upper letter signifies the style of the
right-angled line. The lower letter signifies the
number of dots.

I = double line
S = bold line
J = dashed line
D = two dots
A = three dots
Z = four dots
C = one dot

Therefore, the code is JD.

Q9 D The upper letter signifies the rotation of the
inner shape. The lower letter signifies the
rotation of the outer shape.

W = inner shape opening at top right
K = inner shape opening at bottom right
N = inner shape opening at top left
O = inner shape opening at bottom left
P = outer shape opening at bottom left
Q = outer shape opening at top right
T = outer shape opening at top left

Therefore, the code is WQ.

Q10 A The upper letter signifies the outer shape. The
lower letter signifies the inner shape.

V = outer pentagon
R = outer hexagon
T = outer square
Y = inner circle
Z = inner triangle
X = inner square
S = inner heart

Therefore, the code is VS.

Test 18

Q1 **E** None of the other figures has an even number of small shapes.

Q2 **D** All of the other figures have two matching concentric large shapes.

Q3 **D** None of the other figures has perpendicular lines and arrowheads on all four line ends.

Q4 **D** All of the other figures have vertical bold lines dividing the rectangle.

Q5 **A** All the other semicircles have a small square which is patterned in the same way as the stripe.

Q6 **B** None of the other figures has a double line in the centre.

Q7 **B** None of the other figures has a bold line on an overlapping edge.

Q8 **A** All of the other figures are identical but rotated and have three white segments.

Q9 **C** All of the other arrows point clockwise.

Q10 **A** All of the other figures have ovals as the innermost shape.

Test 19

Q1 **C** Each figure on the left has two bold lines, one of which touches one corner exactly.

Therefore, the answer is C.

Q2 **B** Each figure on the left is a shape with one curved side. The number of parallel lines inside the shape matches the number of straight sides. The dot is at the junction of two straight lines.

Therefore, the answer is B.

Q3 **A** Each figure on the left consists of two different overlapping shapes with the same number of sides.

Therefore, the answer is A.

Q4 **D** Each figure on the left consists of a white shape with the same shape behind it, shaded black and with a different size and orientation.

Therefore, the answer is D.

Q5 **B** Each figure on the left consists of parallel curved lines. There are two white dots and one black square between them. There is also a bold perpendicular rectangle at the uppermost end. The parallel lines extend beyond the inner shapes in each figure.

Therefore, the answer is B.

Q6 **E** Each figure on the left is an irregular heptagon with two black triangles on opposite sides.

Therefore, the answer is E.

Q7 **C** Each figure on the left is a shape with dotted or dashed lines dividing it exactly in half. There are one or more black dots in one half.

Therefore, the answer is C.

Q8 **E** Each figure on the left is a circle with a rectangle, oval and square inside. The rectangle is shaded with diagonal stripes from top right to bottom left. The oval and square have identical shading.

Therefore, the answer is E.

Q9 **A** Each figure on the left is a shape with arrowheads inside. The number of arrowheads matches the number of sides of the shape.

Therefore, the answer is A.

Q10 **D** Each figure on the left is a square with inset corners and a line dividing it exactly in half. It contains three identical shapes with two on one side of the line and one on the other. The shapes on opposite sides have different shading.

Therefore, the answer is D.

Test 20

Q1 **B** The first letter signifies the inner shape. The second letter signifies the outer shape.

B = inner circle
P = inner square
R = inner triangle
X = outer square
Y = outer triangle

Therefore, the code is RY.

Q2 **A** The first letter signifies the location of the line. The second letter signifies the style of the line.

N = bottom left
Q = top right
Z = top left
V = bold line
X = double line

Therefore, the code is QV.

Q3 **D** The first letter signifies the central shape. The second letter signifies the direction of the arrow. The third letter signifies the shading of the central shape.

O = triangle
D = square

C = circle
Z = arrow pointing clockwise
P = arrow pointing anticlockwise
A = black shading
B = vertical striped shading

Therefore, the code is CZB.

Q4 A The first letter signifies the type of small shape. The second letter signifies whether the shapes are in the top half or lower half. The third letter signifies the number of small shapes.

F = squares
J = circles
G = shapes in the lower half
N = shapes in the top half
H = three shapes
I = two shapes

Therefore, the code is JGH.

Q5 E The first letter signifies the shading of the arrows. The second letter signifies the orientation of the arrows.

L = white
F = black
I = points upwards
Q = points right
K = points downwards
O = points left

Therefore, the code is FI.

Q6 A The first letter signifies the orientation of the square. The second letter signifies the shading of the square.

M = square parallel with the outer square
V = square at an angle to outer square
S = vertical, dotted, horizontal and white shading
P = dotted, crosshatched, black and vertical shading
T = black, diagonal, diagonal and white shading

Therefore, the code is MP.

Q7 E The first letter signifies the number of small triangles shaded. The second letter signifies the orientation of the large triangle.

R = three small triangles shaded black
W = no small triangles shaded
T = one small triangle shaded black
V = triangle pointing upwards
Y = triangle pointing downwards

Therefore, the code is RY.

Q8 D The first letter signifies the shading of the small shapes. The second letter signifies the style of the horizontal line. The third letter signifies the type of small shape.

M = white and black shading
R = both shapes white
P = both shapes black
O = bold horizontal line
F = dashed horizontal line
J = dotted horizontal line
C = two small triangles
D = two small circles
E = two small squares
N = two small rectangles

Therefore, the code is MOE.

Q9 D The first letter signifies the shading of the front face of the cube. The second letter signifies the orientation of the cube.

A = cross
P = black shading
Q = no shading
V = front face on left
B = front face on right

Therefore, the code is QB.

Q10 A The first letter signifies the style of line within the semicircle. The second letter signifies the position of the semicircle.

C = double line
S = dashed line
D = dotted line
R = semicircle on the left
L = semicircle at the top
F = semicircle at the bottom
W = semicircle on the right

Therefore, the code is SF.

Test 21

Q1 B Each figure on the left is a triangle with one concave curved shape cut out of it. There are two black dots and one white dot.

Therefore, the answer is B.

Q2 C Each figure on the left is a right-angled triangle with one dashed side opposite the right angle.

Therefore, the answer is C.

Q3 C Each figure on the left is a shape containing crossed arrows. One arrowhead is bold and the other is fine.

Therefore, the answer is C.

Test 21 answers continue on next page

Q4 **A** Each figure on the left is a symmetrical shape with a bold line at the top and a line dividing it down the centre. There is a white shape on the left-hand side and a black shape on the right-hand side. All white shapes have single outlines.

Therefore, the answer is A.

Q5 **A** Each figure on the left consists of a straight line with matching shapes at each end, one white and one black. Crossing the straight line at different angles (not parallel) is one dashed line and one solid line.

Therefore, the answer is A.

Q6 **E** Each figure on the left is an irregular pentagon with one black dot in the top right-hand corner and four short, vertical, parallel lines inside.

Therefore, the answer is E.

Q7 **B** Each figure on the left is a symmetrical shape with a circle inside. One element of the circle's shading is outside the circle.

Therefore, the answer is B.

Q8 **A** Each figure on the left is a square with the bottom right corner shaded. There is an arrow with a line that matches the shading outside the square. It runs along the opposite two sides and points clockwise.

Therefore, the answer is A.

Q9 **B** Each figure on the left consists of three identical shapes. The top left-hand shape is white, the top right-hand shape is diagonally shaded from top right to bottom left and the lower shape is shaded black.

Therefore, the answer is B.

Q10 **E** Each figure on the left is a hexagon with a wavy line dividing it exactly in half.

Therefore, the answer is E.

Q11 **E** Each figure on the left consists of three lines with three small shapes. The lines do not cross.

Therefore, the answer is E.

Q12 **A** Each figure on the left consists of two matching concentric shapes divided exactly in half. Alternating sections are shaded black and white.

Therefore, the answer is A.

Test 22

Q1 **B** Moving from left to right, each pair of triangles is identical, with the upper triangle rotated through 180°.

Therefore, the answer is B.

Q2 **C** All the upper triangles contain two small rectangles and two short horizontal lines in the same positions. All the lower triangles contain two small squares and one short horizontal line in the same positions. Moving from left to right, the uppermost small shapes in each pair of triangles have the same shading.

Therefore, the answer is C.

Q3 **A** Moving from left to right, the arrowheads in the lower triangles all move one place downwards each time. The arrowheads in the upper triangles all move one place upwards.

Therefore, the answer is A.

Q4 **E** Moving from left to right, the lower triangles all have vertical shading in the bottom stripe and one additional concentric circle each time. The upper triangles all have horizontal shading in the upper stripe and one additional concentric square each time.

Therefore, the answer is E.

Q5 **C** Moving from left to right, each triangle has one line more and one dot fewer than the figure before. Two dots in each triangle touch the lines.

Therefore, the answer is C.

Q6 **A** Moving from left to right, the middle shape in each triangle becomes the two outer shapes in the next triangle.

Therefore, the answer is A.

Q7 **D** Moving from left to right, the line on the upper arc moves one place to the right and the line on the lower arc moves one place to the left. The lower triangles have white dots and the upper triangles have black dots.

Therefore, the answer is D.

Q8 **B** Moving from left to right, the circles rotate one position clockwise each time. In each triangle, the black shape overlaps the grey, which overlaps the white.

Therefore, the answer is B.

Q9 **C** Moving from left to right, the arrow rotates 90° clockwise each time. The line at the end of the arrow alternates between one and two lines.

Therefore, the answer is C.

Q10 **C** The black shaded area is on the left in all upper triangles and on the right in all lower triangles. Moving from left to right, the number of horizontal lines in the lower triangles reduces by one each time and the number of horizontal lines in the upper triangles reduces by one each time.

Therefore, the answer is C.

Q11 **E** Moving from left to right, the number of sections in the circle increases by one each time. The plus sign alternates between being circled and freestanding.

Therefore, the answer is E.

Q12 **A** Moving from left to right, the number of sides in each polygon increases by one. The upper triangles all contain upright bold crosses. The lower triangles all contain angled fine crosses.

Therefore, the answer is A.

Test 23

Q1 **C** In each line from point to point, the figures are identical but the shading alternates.

Therefore, the missing triangle should contain a small black arch shape inside a large white one in the bottom right corner.

Therefore, the answer is C.

Q2 **D** In each pair of inner and outer triangles, the striped sections are on the same side. In the outer triangles, the number of crosses follows the sequence: one, two, three. The inner triangles have dots that alternate between black and white and follow the sequence: one, two, three.

Therefore, the missing triangle should contain one cross and the upper section of the left-hand corner should be striped.

Therefore, the answer is D.

Q3 **E** Each inner triangle reflects the outer triangle, but with dots at the ends of each line and a central, perpendicular line added.

Therefore, the missing triangle should contain three parallel lines with a dot at either end and a central, perpendicular line.

Therefore, the answer is E.

Q4 **A** The shapes in the inner and outer triangles are identical but with reversed shading.

Therefore, the missing triangle should consist of a diamond with the left side shaded black.

Therefore, the answer is A.

Q5 **B** Each line from point to point contains the same shield shape. All the shields point inwards. The outer shield shape is bold.

Therefore, the missing triangle should contain a shield with a concave curved top and bold outline. It should point towards the left side of the triangle.

Therefore, the answer is B.

Q6 **B** In each diagonal line of triangles from top right to bottom left, the figures are identical (all triangles or all four-petalled flowers). In diagonal lines of triangles from top left to bottom right, the shading is identical (all black or all white). In the outer triangles, the dots are in the outer points and follow the sequence: one, two, three. In the inner triangles, the dots are in the inner points and follow the sequence: one, two, three.

Therefore, the missing triangle should contain a four-petalled flower, shaded black, with one dot in the lower left-hand corner.

Therefore, the answer is B.

Q7 **A** In the diagonal lines from top right to bottom left, all the triangles have the same shading (vertical or horizontal stripes). Moving anticlockwise around the outer triangles, the rectangles become smaller each time, with all the rectangles orientated inward. Moving anticlockwise round the inner triangles, the circles become larger each time.

Therefore, the missing triangle should have vertical stripes and a large black circle.

Therefore, the answer is A.

Q8 **C** The outer triangles all contain semicircles with black and white sections. Each outer triangle has the same number of arrowheads (curved and unattached) as the inner triangle (straight and attached).

Therefore, the missing triangle should contain a semicircle, with black shading to the right, and four curved arrowheads.

Therefore, the answer is C.

Test 23 answers continue on next page

Q9 A Moving anticlockwise, the outer triangles contain a decreasing number of dots starting from the uppermost triangle. Moving anticlockwise, the inner triangles contain an increasing number of crosses from the uppermost triangle. One cross in every inner triangle is bold and one dot in every outer triangle is shaded black.

Therefore, the missing figure should consist of three crosses, one of which is bold.

Therefore, the answer is A.

Q10 E Each vertical column contains identical double-lined shapes. Each horizontal row contains inner shapes with identical shading.

Therefore, the missing triangle should contain a double-lined triangle pointing upwards with a white inner triangle.

Therefore, the answer is E.

Q11 A The black shapes in the inner triangles are the same as those in the outer triangles, but with the rest of the circle removed.

Therefore, the missing triangle should contain two eighths of a circle shaded (at ten o'clock and two o'clock) with the rest of the circle removed.

Therefore, the answer is A.

Q12 D Each inner triangle is a mirror image of the outer triangle but with the shading reversed.

Therefore, the missing triangle should contain a triangular stack of six squares. The three squares at the outer points of the triangle should be shaded black.

Therefore, the answer is D.

Test 24

Q1 A Moving from the left to the right triangle, the arc is duplicated and both arcs are aligned in parallel. In the lower row of triangles the inner arcs are made bold.

Therefore, the answer is A.

Q2 E Moving from the left to the right triangle, the number of crosses on the left corresponds with the number of sides of the regular shape on the right.

Therefore, the answer is E.

Q3 C Moving from the left to the right triangle, each shape becomes small and black. It is duplicated the same number of times as there are vertical stripes.

Therefore, the answer is C.

Q4 D Moving from the left to the right triangle, the two small shaded triangles within each of the four larger triangles are reversed.

Therefore, the answer is D.

Q5 E Each shape in the triangle on the right is the mirror image of the corresponding shape in the triangle on the left, but the shape is shaded black.

Therefore, the answer is E.

Q6 B Moving from the left to the right triangle, the horizontal lines are bordered on each side by vertical lines to create a striped rectangle. To the left of the new rectangle, there is a parallel, downward-pointing arrow with a black arrowhead. It is the same length as the rectangle exactly.

Therefore, the answer is B.

Q7 B Moving from the left to the right triangle, the shapes on each vertical line move one position downwards.

Therefore, the answer is B.

Q8 E Moving from the left to the right triangle, the dot or line at the centre of each shape becomes the line style for the outer shape.

Therefore, the answer is E.

Q9 A Moving from the left to the right triangle, the arrow in each triangle reverses direction and the line styles of the small shape and arrowhead are reversed.

Therefore, the answer is A.

Q10 B Moving from the left to the right triangle, the two shapes join together.

Therefore, the answer is B.

Q11 B Moving from the left to the right triangle, the shape in each triangle is rotated 180°.

Therefore, the answer is B.

Q12 D Moving from the left to the right triangle, the horizontal lines become bold and the upper bracket is rotated 180°.

Therefore, the answer is D.